Careers in Asset Management and Retail Brokerage

2007 Edition

WetFeet Insider Guide

Helping you make smarter career decisions.

WetFeet, Inc.

The Folger Building
101 Howard Street
Suite 300
San Francisco, CA 94105

Phone: (415) 284-7900 or 1-800-926-4JOB
Fax: (415) 284-7910
Website: www.wetfeet.com

Careers in Asset Management and Retail Brokerage

2007 Edition
ISBN: 978-1-58207-648-5

Table of Contents

Asset Management and Retail Brokerage at a Glance

Opportunity Overview

- Undergrads from all majors are recruited to work in operations, research, trading, customer service, marketing, and sales. Positions with direct customer contact usually require licenses. Undergrads are rarely accepted into retail brokerage training programs, which are usually reserved for midcareer professionals.

- Hot talent right out of business school may come in as portfolio managers, but more likely they will start as assistant managers, researchers, and analysts, providing support and resources for decision makers. Some eventually become fund managers. Retail brokerage jobs also require relevant real-world experience.

- Midcareer professionals with experience in direct mail, advertising, bank operations, communications, data processing, retailing, and other customer service industries can find midlevel jobs at mutual funds and other asset management companies. Retail brokerage houses will consider midcareer professionals as brokers; these pros are usually in their 30s to early 40s, with proven success in other fields.

Major Pluses about Careers in This Industry

- Generous compensation

- High visibility, particularly for fund managers

- Dynamic environment that changes with daily market fluctuations

- Merit-based: If you're good at making money for investors, you can make lots for yourself.

- The satisfaction of helping people achieve financial security

- Excellent benefits and vacation packages

- Abundant holidays, compliments of the New York Stock Exchange

- Management ranks are ripe for a shift as baby boomer senior execs get ready to take their bull market winnings and retire.

Major Minuses about Careers in This Industry

- Vulnerability to business and stock market cycles

- Increased regulations in the wake of trading scandals make day-to-day work more complicated at the very least.

- Highly structured environment in larger firms makes it easy to feel slotted or pigeonholed.

- Grueling hours in the retail brokerage industry

- As long as your clients' money is in the market, you're working—regardless of vacations, sick days, or your best friend's wedding.

Recruiting Overview

- The recruiting process is formal and highly competitive for portfolio managers and the analyst jobs that lead up to them. It's less formal but still very selective for other positions.

- There is a variety of channels to jobs in the industry, from campus recruiting for analysts and private client positions to job searches through the Internet or via headhunters. Networking is usually the key to finding a job at a hedge fund.

- The industry has largely recovered from the twin blows of the bear market and the financial-sector scandals of the early years of the new millennium. Recruiters are hiring, albeit at a guarded pace compared to the boom-boom years of the late 1990s.

- Brokerage training programs at top-tier firms are often closed to most undergrads and MBAs. Midcareer professionals with solid experience and contacts have a better chance of securing a place in this type of program.

- Candidates with top-shelf analytical skills accompanied by technical skills are in demand.

- The industry seeks out non-MBA advanced-degree holders, especially those with math, statistics, and physics PhDs, for positions as quantitative analysts.

- The hedge fund sector has grown rapidly, driven by outsized performance gains. Competition for these spots is fierce, even as returns appear to slow.

The Industries

Overview

"Because that is where the money is." Willy Sutton's immortal reply to the reporter who asked him why he robbed banks might also explain why people go into the asset management and retail brokerage industries. Indeed, companies such as State Street Global Advisors, Barclays Global Investors, and Fidelity Investments each had in excess of $1 trillion in client assets under management at the end of March 2006. And over in the brokerage sector, Merrill Lynch, Smith Barney, and Charles Schwab each had over $1 trillion in client assets at the start of 2006. A host of other asset management and brokerage firms are nipping at the heels of these companies.

Asset management and retail brokerage firms are in the business of using money to make more of it. In the process, many people who work in the industry make a lot of it for themselves, too. Moreover, though they do it with hard work and intensity, many people in the industry successfully avoid the death-march common in investment banking and management consulting.

Asset management companies manage the money of their clients to achieve specific financial objectives within guidelines under which the investment pool is organized. The pool might take the form of a mutual fund, hedge fund, retirement or pension fund, or other institutional fund and, depending on how the fund is organized, could invest in any range of investment vehicles including equities, fixed-income securities, and derivative products such as options and futures.

As a retail stockbroker or financial advisor, you provide much the same function as asset managers: picking stocks, bonds, and other investments, determining the right portfolio mix, executing trades, and ultimately increasing or preserving wealth—albeit on a smaller scale and with fewer investment tools at your disposal—for individual investors.

The asset management juggernaut requires an equally enormous infrastructure. For every fund, there is not only a fund manager, but also a team of analysts to research equities and fixed-income investments, economists and other soothsayers to augur the direction of the market and economy, salespeople and marketers to get people to buy the fund, traders to execute orders, accountants to track assets, and legions of tech specialists and back-office staff. There's a similar infrastructure for retail brokerages. Ultimately, all these people are trying to make money for their clients and themselves.

 **INSIDER TIP**

The industry may never again see the growth in client assets and hiring that it did in the 1990s. But the biggest firms continue to cull the best and brightest from each year's graduating class, and some expect that by the end of 2006, firms will have taken on more staff than the year before.

Anyone considering a career in asset management or retail brokerage should be keenly aware that markets not only go up, but also go down—sometimes way down. There was a time, in another century, when the markets were on a rocket ship to the moon. The year was 1999 and the entire financial services industry was, well, partying like it was 1999. Suburbanites dropping the kids off to school in their Dodge Caravans spoke about stocks with a passion they had hitherto reserved for Oprah's Book Club selections. Everyone was a financial genius—not just brokers and fund managers. Even pimply-faced kids in junior high were expert stock pickers.

The hangover from all that partying made the financial services industry a much soberer place. The rookies were largely sidelined, and investments became once again the bailiwick of professionals. But the stock market has made a comeback in recent years. As of May 18, 2006, for instance, the Dow Jones Industrial Average was at 11,155, up 53 percent from its post-bust low of 7,286 in October 2002—but still below its January 2000 peak of 11,720. The S&P 500 Index (a broader look at market performance), meanwhile, clocked in at 1,265, up 63 percent from its post-bust low of 777 in October 2002—but, again, still lower than its peak during the boom, 1,527 in March 2000. As the market has improved, more money has poured into asset management and brokerage accounts. Indeed, stock-based mutual funds took in $177.5 billion in net assets in 2004, up 17 percent from the previous year and the largest annual inflow since 2000, says the Investment Company Institute (ICI). And in 2005, net assets in stock-based mutual funds increased by another $135.6 billion. Almost all the asset management and brokerage firms this guide tracks showed an increase in client assets in 2005 (see the tables in the "Industry Rankings" section).

The asset management and brokerage sectors are home to tons of jobs. According to the ICI, 146,250 people worked in the mutual funds sector at the end of 2005. That's a lot of jobs. And in the securities industry overall, 795,700 people were employed at the end of February 2006, up 44,700 from the industry's employment-level nadir in October 2003. In other words, companies are hiring. But the industry has only recovered about half of the 89,900 jobs it lost starting in March 2001, so don't expect companies to be hiring at the same breakneck rate they were in the late 1990s.

Amidst the broken chandeliers and shattered vases of the postbubble financial industry, some potentially exceptional opportunities still exist. "I'd expect growth in the industry to be as fast [as] or faster than employment growth in the general economy," says one recruiter. And if you do manage to find (and keep) a job in the industry, you can still expect to make a solid living and retain something of a life, particularly compared to the slave-labor existence of your investment banking peers.

The Bottom Line

With the tremendous proliferation of 401(k), IRA, and other types of retirement plans during the 1990s, more people than ever before can now be classified as investors. An estimated 91 million individuals in 54 million households, or nearly half of all U.S. households, owned mutual funds in 2005, says the ICI. The choices for the small-time investor have never been greater, including stocks, bonds, mutual funds, real estate trusts, exchange-traded funds (ETFs), and options. There's also a range of venues available should one have an itch to invest, including traditional full-service firms, discount brokerages, and do-it-yourself online trading. And we haven't even considered the institutional investor yet. The pensions, insurance companies, corporations, foundations, and endowments that used to comprise nearly all investors are still around, and money managers are still there to try to create wealth for them.

This all boils down to a wide range of career options in a dynamic industry. What's in demand is closely tied to a firm's strategy. Discount brokers, the ones that benefited the most from average Joe day trading, have kept a tight cap on headcount now that Joe has gone back to his day job. The largest, generally New York–based, brokerage houses (sometimes called *wirehouses*) continue to recruit trainees for number-crunching analyst positions and more sales-oriented marketing and brokerage support jobs. And the merger frenzy that took hold of the financial services sector in the late 1990s and early part of this decade has endowed some regional players with bigger aspirations. Wachovia Securities, for instance—created by the 2003 merger of the brokerage arms of Wachovia Corp. and Prudential Financial—has been aggressive in ramping up its brokerage operation in recent times.

Industry Breakdown

Asset management companies and retail brokerages occupy only a part of the matrix that is the financial services industry. Nevertheless, it's worth looking at the industry as a whole for a few reasons. First, it's helpful to know what retail brokerages and asset management firms are *not*. Next, the boundaries between different sectors in the industry often blur, with firms in one sector participating in the activities of another. Finally, as the industry goes through its current consolidation phase, firms that once occupied different places in the landscape now find themselves under the same roof.

Many leading full-service financial institutions now have investment banking and retail brokerage arms. Citigroup became a top-tier investment banking player when it merged with Travelers and its Salomon Smith Barney subsidiary back in 1998; Chase, when it acquired J.P. Morgan in 2000. Investment bankers essentially help corporations issue debt or equity securities. An obvious example is the investment bank that underwrites an initial public offering (IPO) for a startup firm. But investment bankers don't stop when the IPOs dry up; they also advise companies on M&A targets, find companies buyers, and help companies meet their capital needs by underwriting secondary public offerings and debt issuances. Investment bankers are the storks that deliver securities to markets.

Brokerages also typically have equity research units made up of analysts and their helpers, who research and recommend stocks to mostly institutional clients rather than individuals. Research drives trading volume and lends investment banks a sense of expertise and authority in the industries in which they specialize. Investment bankers are usually closely allied with capital markets units of major brokerage houses. Capital markets operations then make markets for the securities that have been issued; that is, they find buyers and sellers for newly issued securities. Capital markets departments typically house a brokerage firm's stock and bond traders. These in turn might sell to any number of other traders who represent retail brokerages, mutual funds, or other institutional investors. Linking up these buyers and sellers are brokers.

Brokerage houses often have retail operations that allow individual investors to buy and sell stocks, bonds, and mutual funds. More often than not, they also have private banking operations that cater to wealthy individuals. Then there are the institutional investors—the asset managers, pension fund managers, and mutual fund managers who invest assets on behalf of their clients. Institutional clients include government or private pension funds, corporate retirement plans, or insurance companies. Alongside these primary functions are a number of support roles, including marketing and sales, back-office operations, and compliance, that, although less glamorous, are no less important to the frictionless turning of the industry.

ASSET MANAGEMENT COMPANIES

Asset managers, also called *investment managers* or *money managers*, are responsible for investing the assets of a group, institution, or individual according to specified management goals. Asset management companies are typically organized around funds and run by portfolio managers. These people have a coterie of analysts to support them. Unlike high-profile sell-side analysts, buy-side analysts—those that support the managers— typically analyze a number of companies across industry groups and don't offer their research outside the company. Additionally, larger funds might have strategic analysts and economists on staff to help predict the market direction for a family of funds. Large money managers also employ traders to execute their purchases and sales of securities. Asset managers sometimes have back-office operations to process orders. Finally, firms have sales and relationship management teams to get the general public or institutional investors to buy their asset management services.

Asset management breaks down into five major categories:

Mutual Fund Management

Mutual fund management involves managing funds (into which individual shareholders and institutions have put money) that invest in a combination of stocks and/or bonds and/or money market instruments according to very specific investment goals, and adhering to strict governance laws. Investors own shares of the mutual fund; they do not directly own the stocks, bonds, or other instruments of which the fund may be composed. Mutual funds are regulated under the Investment Company Act of 1940. True mutual funds are considered open-ended; that is, investors can buy or sell shares at any time based on the value of the assets at that time. Closely related to mutual funds are closed-end funds, which offer a fixed number of shares; ETFs, which trade on major exchanges; and unit investment trusts, which offer dividends or interest to their shareholders and have set termination dates.

Modern mutual funds got their American start in 1924 when George Putnam, of the eponymous firm, offered a diversified portfolio of stocks and bonds to the public. Mutual funds have become increasingly popular over the last 15 years, rising in number from 3,079 in 1990 to 8,454 at the end of 2005. Major players in the mutual fund industry include Fidelity Investments, The Vanguard Group, State Street, American Funds (a subsidiary of The Capital Group), and Legg Mason.

Retail Asset Management

Retail asset management includes a host of services, primarily for high-net-worth individuals, that includes trusts and professionally managed accounts (you consent to leave the investment decisions to the professionals). A client's net worth or level of investable assets usually determines the level of service he or she receives, from call center to personal banker. Those that cater to high-net-worth clients tend to offer more exotic investments, such as private equity funds, in part because they're not restricted by regulations designed to protect smaller nest eggs from risky investments. Unlike commission-based brokerage accounts, retail asset managers usually charge a fee based on a percentage of assets under management. Major brokerage houses, such as Merrill Lynch and Morgan Stanley, and many specialized asset management companies offer retail asset management services.

Hedge Fund Management

Much of the public perception of hedge funds is replete with images of elitist investment cabals domiciled on the Gold Coast of Connecticut that make their clients fabulously wealthy through byzantine investment instruments—which is precisely what makes hedge funds so alluring. Because they work outside many of the SEC regulatory and reporting strictures that are imposed on mutual funds, hedge funds are often open only to institutional and accredited investors (generally people with a net worth of more than $1,000,000 or annual household incomes of more than $200,000). The trend has been to democratize funds; some have lowered investment minimums to $25,000. These still have the same freedom to use instruments such as derivatives, leverage, and shorting. The latter, which involves betting that a stock will go down, gives hedge funds an edge during a bear cycle. "Because they don't short, mutual funds are more exposed to the market's ups and downs," says one hedge fund employee.

Their flexibility translated into some hefty returns during the stock market's early 2000s swoon. But average hedge fund performance has dimmed somewhat over the past couple of years, perhaps because there are more and more players having a go at the same game. "You have more people trying to do it—there's a natural bias toward mediocrity," says one industry observer. Indeed, at the end of 2005, there were about 8,500 hedge funds, up 6 percent from the previous year. And after rising by 18.6 percent in 2003, the Greenwich–Van Global Hedge Fund Index posted more modest gains of 7.7 percent and 8.6 percent in 2004 and 2005. More modest returns haven't dissuaded wealthy individuals from the belief that hedge funds are the next best thing since Tiffany's small blue boxes: Assets in hedge funds rose 13 percent in 2005, to $1.13 trillion.

These investment vehicles are popular with their managers, too. In addition to a management fee based on a percentage of assets managed, fund managers receive enormous incentive compensation based on the (positive) returns of the fund. A fund manager typically receives a management fee of 1 to 2 percent of assets along with 20 percent of overall profits. This arrangement is called "one and twenty" in the industry. However, some funds have built-in clauses that ensure that they only pay out the percentage of profits for aggregate gains. That is, if a firm loses money one year, the manager doesn't see a percentage of profits until the fund's gains have surpassed its losses. In addition to fees and a percentage of profits, fund managers typically have their own money invested in these funds, which certainly allies their interests with those of their investors. Larger hedge fund companies include Pequot Capital Management, Tremont Capital Management (a subsidiary of OppenheimerFunds), and Andor Capital Management. Many leading brokerage firms and asset management companies also have these alternative investment products.

Institutional Asset Management

Institutional asset managers invest money on behalf of corporations, insurance companies, pension funds, endowments, and charitable foundations. Asset managers offer this wide range of clientele a picnic basket full of investment goodies, including money market funds, equity investments, fixed-income products, 401(k) and 403(b) administration, and active and indexed funds.

Pension and Retirement Fund Management

Pension and retirement fund management is exactly what the name implies. Back in the good old days when workers didn't have to fund their own retirement plans through 401(k)s and IRAs, employers used to set money aside for their employees' retirement. Ah, how times have changed. Nevertheless, pension funds do still exist; the largest of these, the California Public Employees' Retirement System (a.k.a. CalPERS), had $207 billion in assets as of the end of March 2006. As you might guess, the most populous states in the union have the largest employee retirement funds; following CalPERS are the California State Teachers' Retirement System (which had $130 billion in assets as of the end of June 2005), and the New York State Common Retirement Fund (which had $126 billion in assets as of the end of June 2006). The largest private pension plan is that of General Motors, with more than $90 billion in assets. Pension plans either invest assets themselves or rely on an institutional advisor to invest for them.

RETAIL BROKERAGES

Retail brokerage firms allow individuals from all walks of life to ride the wild roller coaster that is the stock market. Retail brokerages make money primarily through commissions on the trades of their clients, though brokerage firms are trying to move their customers to fee-based management. The retail brokerage industry includes not only full-service brokers such as Merrill Lynch and Morgan Stanley but also a number of discount and online brokers as well as the rarefied realm of private client services or private banking. In recent years, everyone has been trying to get a piece of the action, and lines between these groups have blurred—Merrill offers online trading, Fidelity Investments has a discount brokerage, and Charles Schwab offers retail asset management for high-net-worth individuals through its U.S. Trust subsidiary.

In addition to brokers, retail brokerage operations include trading desks, back-office operations to process transactions, compliance officers to ensure that traders and brokers don't engage in illegal activity, and research departments. Note, though, that most of the sell-side research at brokerage firms is in support of the capital markets units. In and of themselves, research departments are often cost centers, a situation underscored by the conflict-of-interest scandal and Wall Street's settlement with corruption-hound Eliot Spitzer. These days, research is pretty much barred from helping investment bankers reel in new clients.

Full-Service Brokerages

Full-service brokerages facilitate securities trading and act as financial advisors for individuals—recommending stocks, allocating asset portfolios, and executing orders. Many banks and financial services firms have acquired brokerage entities to become one-stop shops for all of an individual's financial needs—personal loans, mortgages, life insurance—in addition to traditional brokerage services. Citigroup, the nation's largest bank, added a full-service brokerage to its product offerings when it merged with Travelers in 1998 and gained Wall Street titan Salomon Smith Barney. Merrill Lynch dominates the industry, with an astonishing $1.8 trillion in client assets and 15,350 financial advisors. Big players here include Merrill Lynch, Citigroup's Smith Barney, Wachovia Securities, and Morgan Stanley.

Discount and Online Brokerages

Charles Schwab pioneered a totally different approach for investors with his experiment in discount brokerages in 1974. Today, Schwab is the world's largest discount brokerage firm. Other firms have followed suit: E-Trade, Ameritrade, and Scottrade offer bare-bones service (no advice, no hand-holding) in exchange for low commissions and technology-rich websites. Today, however, the skies look pretty gray for discount brokerages. As firms such as Merrill Lynch offer fixed-price online trading, companies such as Fidelity expand into the low-end brokerage market, and assets of young investors trickle to a halt, the industry continues onward with consolidation and restructuring. Ameritrade purchased Datek in 2002 to shore up its position in a dwindling market, then grew even larger in 2006 with the acquisition of TD Waterhouse's U.S. operations. Schwab has moved away from its discount roots and has begun offering full-service features to wealthy investors through its acquisition of U.S. Trust. Meanwhile, the major firms have become engaged in a price war, slashing per-trade fees for what is essentially a commodities business: online stock trades.

Private Client Services

Private client services are the gravy train of top-tier brokerage houses. Even Goldman Sachs, best known for advising corporations on big mergers and IPOs, extends its Midas touch to wealthy individuals through its private client services operation. Private client services groups, like full-service retail brokerages, offer investors a full plate of investment vehicles to meet their individual needs. However, unlike ordinary investors, wealthy investors (usually accredited investors) are able to invest in a wide range of unregulated securities and investment devices. The ante that investors need to pony up to get into private banking varies. Those catering to the "ultra-high-net-worth" set keep out the hoi polloi with asset requirements of $25 million. Other firms court the McMansion set, requiring its clients to lay down a mere $500,000. Firms typically charge a management fee as a percentage of this service rather than a commission.

Unlike most retail brokerages, private banks regularly recruit newly minted MBAs. Top private bankers include UBS Private Banking, Goldman Sachs, Merrill Lynch, Morgan Stanley, Credit Suisse, JPMorgan Chase, Citigroup Private Bank, and Neuberger Berman.

INDEPENDENT RESEARCH COMPANIES

One man's tragedy is another man's opportunity. With the besmirching of the reputations of the investment bank–affiliated brokerage houses, independent equity research companies, whose opinions are not influenced by I-banking prerogatives, are getting a boost. Independent research firms fill their ranks with teams of bond analysts as well as analysts who evaluate companies in a variety of industries. As research analysis requires insight into the industry as much as it does an understanding of finance principles, companies often look for people with industry experience. Research companies typically split along the lines of the client base; they cater either to the institutional or the individual investor, with far more firms specializing in institutional research. For the most part, independent firms sell their research on a subscription basis.

Sanford C. Bernstein & Co., now a subsidiary of AllianceBernstein, LP, leads the pack of institutional investor–oriented research firms. Other companies servicing the segment include Sidoti & Co., Argus Research, Equity Research Associates, Vista Research, and CFRA (the Center for Financial Research & Analysis). Firms serving individual investors include Value Line, Weiss Ratings, and Morningstar. Most independent researchers run on a pretty small scale. Even the largest firms such as Value Line and Sidoti only employ 70 and 40 analysts, respectively.

Industry Rankings

Largest Asset Management Companies, as of March 31, 2006

Rank	Company	Assets Under Management ($M)	1-Yr. Change (%)
1	State Street Global Advisors	1,500,000	12
2	Barclays Global Investors[1]	1,500,000	10
3	Fidelity Investments	1,200,000	9
4	Vanguard Group	980,000	19
5	JPMorgan Asset Management	873,000	10
6	Legg Mason	868,000	132
7	Capital Group[1]	750,000	25
8	Northern Trust Global Investments	653,000	11
9	Credit Suisse Asset Management	619,600	n/a
10	UBS Global Asset Management	614,000	16
11	PIMCO	610,500	37
12	AllianceBernstein	603,000	12
13	Merrill Lynch Investment Managers*	581,000	27
14	Goldman Sachs Asset Management[2]	571,000	23
15	Prudential Financial	547,000	10
16	Wellington Management Co.	542,000	15
17	AIG Global Investment Group	533,000	8
18	MetLife	499,000	37
19	Franklin Templeton Investments	491,600	19
20	BlackRock*	463,000	18

[1]As of December 31, 2005
[2]As of February 28, 2006
*BlackRock and Merrill Lynch Investment Managers announced they're merging in 2006; their combined assets would put the new company in the top five among asset managers, based on client assets under management.
Note: Fidelity, only mutual fund assets under management
Sources: Company reports; WetFeet analysis

Largest Retail Brokerage Companies

Firm	2005 Client Assets ($M)	1-Yr. Change (%)	2005 Revenue ($M)	Financial Advisors
Merrill Lynch GPC	1,473,000	9	10,764	15,160
Charles Schwab	1,199,000	11	4,464	n/a
Smith Barney (a subsidiary of Citigroup)	1,130,000	16	6,825	13,414
Wachovia Securities	683,600	5	5,019	10,500
UBS Wealth Management	673,000	22	5,156	7,520
Fidelity Personal Investments	664,200	13	n/a	n/a
Morgan Stanley[1]	617,000	2	5,019	9,500
Edward Jones	357,000	43	2,891	9,700
A.G. Edwards[2]	343,000	10	2,740	7,000
Ameriprise	264,000	3	5,024	12,000
TDAmeritrade[3]	262,900	n/a	1,003	n/a
E-Trade	179,000	79	1,704	n/a
Raymond James & Associates	150,000	10	1,337	4,886

[1]As of November 30, 2005
[2]As of February 28, 2006
[3]As of March 31, 2006
Sources: Company websites and SEC filings; WetFeet analysis; Hoover's

Industry Trends

COMMISSIONS TO FEES

The retail brokerage industry is weaning itself from its traditional reliance on trade-based commissions by offering more and more fee-based services, which provide a more regular revenue stream in a volatile market. The fee structure also helps insulate firms from appearances of conflicts of interest as the fee is usually a percentage of assets under management, which means that it's in everyone's interest to see those assets grow. Firms usually charge investors 1.1 to 1.5 percent of assets, according to Cerulli Associates. Fees represent a growing slice of the industry's top-line income: At the beginning of the decade, fees accounted for less than 10 percent of revenue; by 2003, they accounted for 25 percent. One observer expects that fees could account for over 70 percent of revenue by decade-end. Moving toward a fee-based model can backfire if it's done without enough customer buy-in, however. In April 2005, the NASD slapped Raymond James Financial with a fine totaling nearly $900,000 for allegedly transferring clients to fee-based accounts without determining whether that was the most appropriate structure for the clients.

SCANDAL DU JOUR: TIMING IS EVERYTHING

The financial services industry hit the Comstock Lode of scandals after the bubble burst, with regulators targeting nearly every corner of Wall Street for working against the best interests of their clients. By 2005, mutual fund firms and brokerages appeared to have put the worst of the probes behind them and were dealing with the fallout. For brokers, that's meant a higher "Chinese wall" between the investment bank and research departments, designed to eliminate the chance that an analyst might tout a company to the public in one breath—thereby pleasing that company's management, which might then push lucrative investment banking business toward the analyst's employer bank—while disparaging the firm in private.

It wasn't just the Armani-pinstripe power broker whose dealings felt the sting of the regulatory whip this decade. The Dockers-wearing mutual fund manager also saw his industry's dirty laundry aired in public, causing massive asset withdrawals at some of the worst culprits. Putnam Investments, Strong Funds, Pilgrim Baxter, and Janus Capital were accused of short-trading in their own funds for certain executives' personal benefit or allowing preferred customers to trade fund shares after hours. The upshot for clients is that fund companies have restricted loosey-goosey trades in mutual funds and generally disclose more to shareholders about how they're spending money, particularly if the commissions that would be generated by these trades could undermine the best price or choice for the investor. The upshot for the industry can be summed up in four words: lawsuits and settlement fees.

THE BROKERAGE MODEL RETHUNK

During the trading frenzy of the late '90s, virtual brokers such as E-Trade and Ameritrade were the vehicles of choice for the savvy day trader. But since the market tumbled, and the average investor realized that he's not the investment genius he thought he was when almost every stock in the market was posting monthly gains, online brokers have had trouble regaining steady and growing trading volume. Investors increasingly appear to be seeking experienced advice and are willing to pay reasonable incremental costs for help in navigating the current turbulent markets.

The result: a strong increase in demand for seasoned brokers. Indeed, because of increased demand, in 2005, 9,071 registered reps changed jobs from one firm to another, up 18 percent from 7,713 in 2004. At Bank of America, for instance, hiring of brokers is up by 40 percent in the first part of 2006 over the same period in 2005. And signing bonuses are soaring; for example, reports claim that Morgan Stanley and UBS are offering signing bonuses to brokers of up to 150 percent of the total commissions and fees they earned in their last year at their old firms.

Some have responded to the changed market-place by consolidating, others by reshuffling management. In recent times, Wachovia and Prudential have formed a brokerage joint venture, Wachovia Securities; Bank of America has purchased FleetBoston and gained its discount brokerage subsidiary Quick & Reilly; Charles Schwab has booted out its long-time CEO and brought back the discount broker's founder; Citigroup has swapped its asset management business for Legg Mason's brokerage business; Merrill Lynch Investment Managers has joined forces with fellow asset management heavyweight BlackRock; Ameritrade has acquired the U.S. operations of TD Waterhouse; and Piper Jaffray has sold its private client services business to UBS.

INSIDER TIP

Brokers and asset managers of all shapes and sizes are looking for professionals who can court and advise well-heeled customers. Just make sure you know your claret from your Beaujolais.

FOLLOW THE MONEY

As smaller investors have shown less of a desire to move their rainy day funds into the stock market since the crash of 2000, brokerages and asset managers have hit on this strategy: Go after the individuals whose nest eggs are so large that they'll look for investment strategies, regardless of what the market is doing. The increasing wealth of the baby boom generation has played a role in this thinking. Nearly every firm has some service targeted at the wealthy, with definitions of "wealthy" ranging from $1 million to $100 million in assets. For more moderate-income customers, the trend has meant saying goodbye to some personalized brokerage services. Merrill Lynch and Morgan Stanley have reportedly tweaked their compensation structure so that brokers get paid less or not at all for handling trades on accounts that fall below a certain asset level, thus discouraging them from taking on smaller customers.

For job seekers, the wealth trend is worth noting because brokers and asset managers of all shapes and sizes are looking for professionals that can court and advise well-heeled customers.

One result of this focus on wooing the wealthy: Brokerages are pushing CFP (Certified Financial Planner) certification among brokers. The thinking goes like this: Unlike many other certifications, the CFP certification is standardized, and it's attractive to wealthy clients because it certifies that its holders have gone through a rigorous training and testing process. Becoming a CFP requires three or more years of work experience, the completion of a financial-planning curriculum at an accredited school, and the completion of a two-day, ten-hour examination, as well as 30 hours of continuing education courses every two years after receiving the CFP.

HEDGING IS THE BET

Once thought arcane, volatile, and the province of Nobel Prize winners such as Myron Scholes, hedge funds have suddenly become arcane, volatile, and wildly popular. Drawn by the potential to make millions, if not tens of millions, each year, MBAs are pounding on the doors of these firms.

Their track record in down markets—hedge funds consistently beat mutual funds when indexes fall—has piqued the interest of smaller investors, even as their records start to look slightly less stellar. The firms, in turn, have noticed. Some hedge funds accept investments as small as $25,000 from individual investors. Asset managers have launched funds of hedge funds—vehicles that use some of the same investing techniques as a traditional hedge fund, such as short-selling, but mitigate the risk by spreading the investment across several hedge funds. Institutional investors such as pension funds and foundations still account for a big part of hedge fund contributions. Regardless of who's investing, hedge fund numbers have grown so much that they now equal the number of mutual funds. Compared to about 100 in the early '90s, investors can now choose from about 8,500 hedge funds.

Hedge funds have seen their share of scandal in recent times. In the past year or so, Bayou Securities has been charged with defrauding investors of $300 million; Millennium Partners has paid a total of $180 million in fines to settle fraud charges; MHC International partners have been accused of fraud for taking fund assets for personal use, for such things as a $160,000 Lamborghini; and International Management Associates has been accused of defrauding investors of some $100 million. (The CEO of International Management Associates went on the lam as a result, but was recently caught in a Miami hotel.)

The Companies

Largest Asset Managers and Mutual Funds

Largest Retail Brokerage Companies

Additional Asset Management Companies

Largest Asset Managers and Mutual Funds

The asset management companies profiled here are listed in alphabetical order. See the "Industry Rankings" section in the previous chapter for tables ranking firms by total assets under management.

ALLIANCEBERNSTEIN LP

1345 Avenue of the Americas
New York, NY 10105
Phone: 212-969-1000
Fax: 212-969-2229
www.alliancebernstein.com

AllianceBernstein is one of the largest investment management companies in the United States, with more than $635 billion assets under management as of April 30, 2006. The acquisition of independent research firm Sanford C. Bernstein in 2000 rounded out Alliance Capital's offerings for private and high-net-worth clients, and complemented the firm's growth-style investing with value-focused products. As of the end of 2005, assets managed for institutions made up 62 percent of client assets. Assets in value-style stocks comprise about 40 percent of the investments made by the firm (compared with just 19 percent in 2000); the rest is allocated to growth stocks and fixed-income securities. The firm is 61 percent owned by AXA, with 32 percent held by the public and the rest by executives and directors.

Headquartered in New York City, AllianceBernstein has a presence in 36 cities worldwide. Its roster includes 4,312 employees, including more than 250 buy-side and more than 100 sell-side research analysts. The firm suffered from the 2003 mutual fund scandal, which caused several company executives to resign, cost the firm $600 million to settle with the SEC, and sent 2003 sales plunging by 40 percent. Its fortunes rebounded in 2004 and 2005.

The firm, which currently has about 260 financial advisors in the U.S., is looking to increase that number by about 10 percent in 2006.

AMERICAN INTERNATIONAL GROUP, INC.

70 Pine Street
New York, NY 10270
Phone: 212-770-7000 or 877-638-4244
Fax: 212-509-9705
www.aig.com

When corruption-hound and New York State Attorney General Eliot Spitzer finished routing out wrongdoing in the mutual fund industry, he turned to the wide but unglamorous field of commercial insurance brokerage. And American International Group, the biggest insurer, was directly in his firing line. The subsequent investigation by the SEC and the state, which focused on whether the firm colluded with insurance brokers engaged in bid-rigging and whether AIG had artificially inflated results, led to big changes at the firm. Its stock plunged and long-time chief Hank Greenberg relinquished his leadership in March 2005. AIG resolved the charges against it in 2006 by agreeing to pay $1.64 billion to the SEC, policyholders, the U.S. Department of Justice, and several states.

Its bruised reputation hasn't lessened the company's overall presence in asset management and brokerage. Its institutional arm, AIG Global Investment Management, manages some $500 billion in assets. On the retail side, AIG has cobbled together a division called AIG Retirement Services. Under that heading fall AIG Annuity Insurance; AIG VALIC (group retirement products); AIG SunAmerica Life Assurance (annuities and asset management); and AIG SunAmerica Asset Management (which manages about $62 billion in client assets in mutual funds). Its broker-dealer affiliates include Advantage Capital (with 400 independent financial advisors), FSC Securities (with 1,700 independent financial professionals), AIG Financial Advisors (with 2,275 independent financial advisors), and Royal Alliance Associates. (AIG's financial advisors are independent contractors—self-employed advisors who use the infrastructure and some of the offerings of broker-dealers like AIG.)

BARCLAYS GLOBAL INVESTORS, N.A.

45 Fremont Street
San Francisco, CA 94105
Phone: 415-597-2000
Fax: 415-597-2271
www.barclaysglobal.com

Barclays Global Investors (BGI) made a name for itself in the '70s when it virtually invented index funds—funds whose holdings are selected by complicated computer models rather than amply paid managers, thus lowering costs. Indexing remains one of the firm's major strategies today, accounting for about two-thirds of its business. But it also manages $357 billion in active and enhanced index funds (as of March 31, 2006). The firm's 2,800 clients include two-thirds of the world's largest 100 pension funds and a third of *Fortune*'s Global 500 companies.

With $1.62 trillion in assets under management (as of March 31, 2006), BGI consistently places among the largest asset management firms in the world. Some of its recent success in attracting client assets comes from the introduction of iShares, its ETFs that allow investors to buy and sell shares in what amounts to a tracking stock for various groups, from Chinese Internet companies to U.S. biotech firms.

Headquartered in San Francisco, BGI's investment researchers also have outposts in London, Tokyo, and Sydney. It also has recently opened client-services offices from Singapore to Amsterdam. Overall, the company—a subsidiary of Britain's Barclays PLC—employs approximately 2,000 people. The research arm, called the Advanced Strategies & Research Group in Barclay lingo, is responsible for creating the entire firm's managed portfolios. Ambitious BA, MBA, and PhD degree candidates might consider applying to a one- to two-year "development programme" that starts the summer before one's final year of study.

BLACKROCK, INC.

40 East 52nd Street
New York, NY 10022
Phone: 212-810-5300
Fax: 212-935-1370
www.blackrock.com

Founded in 1998, BlackRock expanded quickly from a boutique advisory firm known for its bond products to a more diversified asset manager and risk advisor; as of March 31, 2006, it had 1,600 employees and $463 billion in assets under management. Part of that expansion included its January 2005 acquisition of MetLife's State Street Research and Management and State Street Realty, which boosted its equity, alternative investments, and hedge fund capabilities.

The really big news, though, is its merger with Merrill Lynch Investment Managers, which was announced early in 2006 and is scheduled to finalize in the third quarter of the year. Combined, the two firms had $1.044 trillion in client assets under management as of March 31, 2006. In other words, the combined firm will be a global top-ten player in the asset management sector, employing some 4,500 people in 18 countries. Merrill Lynch will have a 50 percent stake in the combined company, which will use the BlackRock name, offer in excess of 250 mutual funds, and benefit from access to the Merrill Lynch distribution network, which comprises more than 15,000 brokers.

BlackRock prides itself on being a technological innovator, using software to analyze securities, assess portfolio risk, and move information. Its success in portfolio analytics, where many of its portfolio managers start, has been such that it's started to sell the analysis to other financial institutions. Employees usually work in one of five areas: asset management, which includes its private client and pension plan teams, portfolio management, global operations, portfolio administration, and BlackRock Solutions, which sells financial-portfolio risk-management technology solutions.

BlackRock recruits mostly from Ivy League universities, big state schools in the Northeast and Southeast, and historically black colleges. But it does encourage candidates from outside its farm schools to email their resumes to careers@blackrock.com.

THE CAPITAL GROUP COMPANIES, INC.

333 South Hope Street
Los Angeles, CA 90071
Phone: 213-486-9200
Fax: 213-486-9217
www.capgroup.com

Haven't heard of The Capital Group? You're not alone. Founded in the dark year 1931, The Capital Group has quietly created the third-largest family of mutual funds in the country—better known as American Funds. American Funds runs six of the ten largest mutual funds in the U.S., and these days its flagship Growth Fund of America is bigger than the giant Vanguard 500 fund. The company encompasses two divisions: Capital Research and Management, the investment advisor to American Funds, and Capital Guardian Trust and Capital International companies, which together provide global investment management services for individuals, corporate retirement plans, and institutional investors. Capital Research's assets under management top $750 billion, while assets managed by Capital Guardian Trust Company and the Capital International companies total about $300 billion. Together, they employ 8,000 people in 21 offices worldwide, including international offices in Montreal, Toronto, London, Geneva, Hong Kong, Singapore, and Tokyo.

The company's lack of publicity says something about its culture as well; The Capital Group is known in the industry for its laid-back attitude and low ego quotient as well as a conservative investment style. Indeed, the company still promotes the values of its founder, Jonathan Bell Lovelace: research-driven investment, long-term focus, and integrity. The company has a very low attrition rate, tends to promote from within, and offers a generous benefits package common to the investment management industry.

The company is under investigation by the SEC and the NASD for allegedly improperly rewarding brokers for pushing its funds. It's in a particularly nasty battle (featuring lawsuits and countersuits) with the attorney general of California—the company doesn't believe he has jurisdiction over its activities.

COLUMBIA MANAGEMENT GROUP

100 Federal Street
Boston, MA 02110
Phone: 617-434-2200
www.columbiamanagement.com

Columbia Management is the newly renamed asset management unit of Bank of America, the Charlotte, North Carolina–based descendent of NationsBank which has been gobbling up regional banks on both coasts. As of mid-2006, it is the country's second-largest bank company by assets. One of its recent conquests, Northeast power-house FleetBoston, came with $160 billion-asset Columbia Management Group, which it combined with its prior asset management operation, Banc of America Capital Management.

The combined asset management group had $361 billion in client assets under management at year-end 2005. Equity investments made up 38 percent of assets, while 47 percent were in money market funds and 15 percent in fixed income. Units within the group include mutual funds under the Columbia and Nations brands, equities, fixed income, quantitative strategies, and product marketing. Portfolio analysts generally work out of Boston, New York, Chicago, and Portland, Oregon.

CREDIT SUISSE ASSET MANAGEMENT SECURITIES, INC.

U.S. Headquarters:
466 Lexington Avenue
New York, NY 10017
Phone: 212-325-2000
Fax: 646-658-0728
www.csam.com

A subsidiary of Swiss-American investment bank Credit Suisse, Credit Suisse Asset Management (CSAM) manages about $620 billion in client assets globally (Credit Suisse recently integrated its asset management into a single global arm). The company came into being in 1997 when Credit Suisse consolidated its 17 boutique asset management companies. In 1999, CSAM acquired Warburg Pincus and folded in Donaldson, Lufkin & Jenrette's asset management arm a year later. The company's platter of investments for institutional and wealthy investors includes hedge funds, private equity, funds of funds, exchange-traded funds, and derivative investments, along with the staple equity and fixed-income products. It engages in both bottom-up investing (which focuses on the fundamentals of specific securities) and top-down investing (which is driven more by macro-economic trends).

CSAM employs people in 18 global locations, but most work in its five core investment centers of London, New York, Zurich, Sydney, and Tokyo. In the United States, CSAM employs about 600 people. CSAM touts its flat management structure (only four promotions before making managing director!) and says it recruits from a wide range of academic backgrounds, since "training on the job is the most effective way to learn, understand, and drive our business."

As part of its effort to expand in Asia, Credit Suisse recently launched a joint venture in South Korea with Woori Asset Management; Credit Suisse has a 30 percent stake in the venture.

DEUTSCHE ASSET MANAGEMENT

U.S. Headquarters:
60 Wall Street, 21st floor
New York, NY 10005
Phone: 212-250-2500
www.deam.com

Deutsche Bank's asset management arm, part of the company's Private Client and Asset Management group, offers both retail and institutional products in the United States and throughout the world. DeAM, as company insiders refer to it, employs more than 5,000 people, including 700 investment professionals, in major financial centers worldwide, and manages $633 billion in assets for clients in more than 48 countries. In Europe, its retail DWS Investments unit controls about 25 percent of the German mutual fund market. In the United States, DeAM fleshed out its financial advisor capabilities when it bought Scudder Investments in 2002 for $2.5 billion; its DWS Scudder subsidiary is its entry in the U.S. mutual funds marketplace.

Deutsche had a leg up on the competition when the real estate market boomed over the past few years. Its RREEF real estate business employs 2,000 real estate professionals who manage high-yielding, proprietary real estate investments and investments in publicly traded real estate investment trusts, or REITs. Assets under management for this business total 53 billion euros.

Parent Deutsche Bank invites undergrad, master's, and PhD candidates to apply to one of its summer or full-time analyst or associate programs.

FIDELITY INVESTMENTS

82 Devonshire Street
Boston, MA 02109
Phone: 617-563-7000
Fax: 617-476-6150
www.fidelity.com

The largest mutual fund manager, if you count money-market mutual funds, and the country's top 401(k) provider, Fidelity has more than $1.2 trillion in mutual fund assets under management and runs more than 300 mutual funds. Once best known for its flagship Magellan Fund, managed by name-brand fund manager Peter Lynch, Fidelity has since spread out to retail brokerage, IRAs, 401(k)s, life insurance, and even startup financing. Like other big fund companies, Fidelity—or Fido, as it's sometimes called in the industry—has been slashing expenses on its index funds in a bid to lure more investors.

In early 2005, Fido announced the spin-off of its institutional arm into a separate firm, which manages more than $100 billion in corporate and public pension assets. Although Fidelity entered 2005 untainted by the fund-trading scandal, it took a blow to its reputation due to a very public scandal involving some of its traders, who improperly accepted gifts from brokers, including a lavish bachelor party (complete with hired dwarfs) that's now notorious on Wall Street. The company reassigned its head of stock trading to a new position as a result, fining him $50,000 to boot. It also disciplined a handful of other employees, some of whom have left the company.

In an effort to improve the performance of its funds, in 2005 the company reorganized to facilitate closer interaction between fund managers, research analysts, and traders working on the same funds. It also launched an effort to double the size of its equity research staff, from 90 research analysts to 180. And it replaced the manager of the Magellan Fund, which has been a market laggard in recent years.

The company is privately held; the Johnson family that founded the firm owns approximately half. Family scion Abigail Johnson owns about a quarter of the company herself and recently switched positions from president of the mutual fund division to president of the retirement division. Its private structure means that Fidelity can spend $700 million on upgrading its online brokerage without worrying about the next quarterly earnings report.

Because the company has a policy of hiring fund managers from within, it views the selection of analysts as critical to its success. Early on, company interviewers plumb applicants' personal interests to find a fit (e.g., a person with a bent for baseball statistics might transfer that interest into evaluating companies). Once in action, analysts have a lot of flexibility in how they choose to pick stocks; the firm believes there's no one perfect investment style.

FRANKLIN TEMPLETON INVESTMENTS

1 Franklin Parkway, Building 970, 1st Floor
San Mateo, CA 94403
Phone: 650-312-2000 or 800-632-2350
Fax: 650-312-5606
www.franklintempleton.com

Franklin Resources, the parent company of Franklin Templeton mutual funds, settled a number of state and regulatory investigations in 2004, and in August of that year agreed to a $50 million settlement over market timing charges. Despite the bad publicity, Franklin—which trades under the clever ticker BEN—managed to increase assets under management from $335 billion at the beginning of 2004 to $492 billion at the end of March 2006. Over the past couple of years it's increased its staff by more than 700; current staff numbers 7,200 people, who work in 29 countries and serve investors in more than 100 countries. Its research team includes more than 35 analysts.

The company's mutual funds run the gamut of traditional investments, from domestic to international, taxable to tax-free, stocks to bonds. The company has been expanding its grasp steadily. In 2000, Franklin bought out a joint venture partner in South Korea, becoming the first fully foreign-owned investment trust management company in the country. That same year, it bought the Canadian company Bissett & Associates Investment Management. In 2001, it acquired Fiduciary Trust, an investment manager for institutions and high-net-worth individuals. In 2003 it acquired Darby Overseas Investments, a niche private equity and mezzanine finance house. And the Indian company Pioneer ITI AMT is another recent acquisition, making Franklin Templeton one of the leading mutual funds companies in India.

The founding Johnson family still owns a big chunk of available shares and holds senior positions: half-brothers Charles and Rupert hold the titles of chairman and vice chairman, respectively, while Charles' son Gregory is co-CEO.

The company offers several ways in if you're working toward your undergraduate or MBA degree. Its two-year research associate program aims to mold its charges into a bona fide stock or bond picker. And remember, it's one of the few big asset management firms where you can enjoy the sunny West Coast lifestyle while making Wall Street bucks.

GOLDMAN SACHS ASSET MANAGEMENT

85 Broad Street

New York, NY 10004

Phone: 212-902-1000

Fax: 212-902-3000

www.gs.com

Goldman Sachs tries to be the gold standard in its main businesses, which include investment banking, trading and principal investments, and investment management. While not as prominent as its investment banking sibling, Goldman Sachs's investment group has built a 24-karat business around U.S.-based and global mutual funds, managed accounts, nontraditional investments and hedge funds, and private equity placements. At the end of February 2006, it had $571 billion in assets under management, 18 percent higher than the year earlier. Investment management includes private wealth management, which advises affluent individuals, and Goldman Sachs Asset Management, which serves pension funds, endowments, and other institutions.

Goldman offers a program for its asset management recruits similar to the one it offers its investment bankers. Undergrads can apply for a two-year financial analyst position in its investment management group. MBA and other advanced-degree holders who have already spent two to five years in the workforce can apply to an associate program. Within the asset management group, jobs include equity research, quantitative resources, bond and currency analysis, and client relationship management. Goldman employs more than 31,000 people around the world.

JPMORGAN ASSET MANAGEMENT HOLDINGS INC.

522 Fifth Avenue
New York, NY 10036
Phone: 212-483-2323
im.jpmorgan.com

JPMorgan Asset Management (the firm was known as J.P. Morgan Fleming Asset Management until very recently), the investment arm of JPMorgan Chase, is a giant begotten of successive mergers. In 2000, Chase Manhattan Bank bought prestigious British investment firm Robert Fleming Holdings. Then Chase merged with J.P. Morgan. Another mega-merger, the 2004 link-up with Chicago-based Bank One, brought One's retail asset management into the JPMorgan fold.

JPMorgan Asset Management now has $873 billion in assets under management and operates the fifth-largest mutual fund complex in the United States. In 2005 its parent sold its discount broker subsidiary, BrownCo.

Candidates with an undergraduate degree and GPA of 3.2 and higher can apply to the three-year analyst program at JPMorgan Funds, which manages 101 funds. New analysts are first immersed in a five-week training program taught by senior Morgan managers and professors. Duties as an analyst include product analysis, stock research, and developing sales and marketing programs.

The company recently acquired a majority interest in the $7 billion hedge fund Highbridge Capital Management. In 2005, it became the largest seller of mutual funds in Europe.

LEGG MASON, INC.

100 Light Street
Baltimore, MD 21202
Phone: 410-539-0000 or 877-534-4627
Fax: 410-454-4923
www.leggmason.com

In 2005, Legg Mason swapped its brokerage operations for Citigroup's asset management business, adding Citi's $437 billion in assets under management to its own already sizeable operations to become an asset management behemoth. The merger moved the company from 28th place among mutual funds companies to 6th place; as of March 31, 2006, it had $868 billion in client assets under management.

Since making the swap, Legg Mason has focused on integrating the pieces of Citi that it picked up in the deal into its existing operations. As part of that process, it recently gave Citigroup Asset Management the new name of ClearBridge Advisors (which has $100 billion in assets under management), and renamed Smith Barney Funds, now called Legg Mason Partners Funds. In addition, it's integrating its technology systems to capture all of the firm's internal research so that all of its investment professionals can share information.

As part of its deal with Citigroup, Legg Mason will be able to use Citi's huge sales force for three years to sell its funds.

Legg Mason, which has 5,580 employees, is known for its conservative, value approach to investing. In its own words, the firm has a "bottom-up, primary research intensive, fundamental approach" to picking investments, with a focus on companies with "solid economic returns relative to their risk-adjusted valuations." It does not have a star culture, and has stated, "We want to move to a partnership-like culture so that the success of the individual isn't solely a function of their job but also a contribution to the overall enterprise."

MORGAN STANLEY INVESTMENT MANAGEMENT

1221 Avenue of the Americas
New York, NY 10020
Phone: 212-762-7100 or 800-422-6464
www.morganstanley.com/im

Morgan Stanley Investment Management handles $442 billion in client assets for a range of institutional clients, including companies, endowments, and unions, as well as individual investors in mutual funds managed by Morgan Stanley Investment Advisors and investors who make investments through other brokerage firms, banks and financial planners via Van Kampen Investments, a wholly owned subsidiary. (As of February 2006, assets under management or supervision included $247 billion in institutional assets and $195 billion in retail assets.)

Morgan Stanley Investment Management is the asset management arm of blue-chip investment bank and brokerage Morgan Stanley. The parent spent much of 2005 embroiled in a management struggle between CEO Philip Purcell, who hailed from the decidedly non-blue-chip Dean Witter brokerage, and former Wall Street deal makers who owned shares in the company and were dissatisfied with Purcell's performance. Ultimately, Purcell was forced out.

Morgan Stanley offers analyst and associate positions in investment management. Both can start in the global investor group; sales and marketing; or operations, risk management, or product development. Associates can also start in the Alternative Investment Partners group, which manages portfolios of investments such as hedge funds for high-net-worth individuals. Analysts with recent BAs or BSs may be located in New York City; West Conshohocken, Pennsylvania; Oak Brook, Illinois; Houston; and Jersey City, New Jersey. The Private Wealth Management Group recruits MBAs for a five-month associate program that begins in New York City.

NORTHERN TRUST CORPORATION

50 South LaSalle Street
Chicago, IL 60675
Phone: 312-630-6000
Fax: 312-630-1512
www.northerntrust.com

Founded in 1889, Northern Trust is one of the old-line wealth managers and spent much of the last century managing the fortunes of rich Midwesterners. It still advises 20 percent of the nation's richest families, including members of the Bush dynasty, according to one report. But Northern Trust has increasingly set its sights overseas. In March 2005 it bought the Financial Services Group (FSG) of London's Baring Asset Management, which had $70 billion in assets under management. Its 8,844 employees (including 785 that came onboard with FSG) work in offices in 18 states and 12 countries. As of March 2006, Northern Trust counted $653 billion in assets under management.

The firm consists of two business units: Personal Financial Services and Corporate and Institutional Services. Personal Financial Services offers trust administration, private banking, residential mortgage lending, and brokerage and investment management services to small businesses and individuals. Corporate and Institutional Services provides trust, global custody, investment retirement, commercial banking, and treasury management services worldwide.

In the United States, the company offers two 15- to 24-month entry-level tracks. The Gold Program prepares new hires for careers in investments, relationship management, credit services, and operations. The portfolio accounting analyst track preps new recruits for jobs in investment accounting and consulting. The company recruits at DePaul, Howard University, Loyola University, Northwestern, the University of Illinois at Chicago, the University of Illinois at Urbana-Champaign, the University of Iowa, the University of Miami, the University of Michigan, and the University of Texas.

PACIFIC INVESTMENT MANAGEMENT COMPANY, LLC (PIMCO)

840 Newport Center Drive, Suite 300
Newport Beach, CA 92660
Phone: 949-720-6000 or 800-746-2602
Fax: 949-720-1376
www.pimco.com

The gentlemen of PIMCO prefer bonds. Away from the hustle and bustle of Wall Street, PIMCO is one of the largest specialists in fixed-income products and has a reputation for knowing what's up when yields drop. Chief Investment Officer Bill Gross frequently appears on all-business cable shows when the Federal Reserve is about to make a rate move. Its PIMCO Total Return Fund is the largest U.S. bond mutual fund.

This Southern California company's preference for bonds has served it well as the equity markets roiled investors. While other money managers lost assets, PIMCO's shot up by more than 25 percent in 2002 and nearly 30 percent in 2003. Growth has slowed somewhat as the equity markets have moved into bull territory. Nonetheless, assets under management climbed 19 percent in 2004 to $445 billion, and another 33 percent in 2005 to $594 billion. The company credits its success to a total return approach and long-term focus. Innovation has helped as well. In order to allay concerns that rising inflation would cut into bond fund returns, PIMCO has rolled out a series of inflation-protected funds.

PIMCO is a subsidiary of Germany's insurance giant Allianz. Although it doesn't have the extensive analyst associate programs of some fund firms, PIMCO does offer a flat organization that grants responsibility early on. PIMCO offers opportunities in its portfolio management, account management, and business management divisions. Besides its home base of Newport Beach, PIMCO has offices in New York, Hong Kong, London, Tokyo, Toronto, Singapore, Sydney, and Munich. It has approximately 775 employees.

PRUDENTIAL FINANCIAL, INC.

751 Broad Street
Newark, NJ 07102
Phone: 973-802-6000 or 800-346-3778
Fax: 973-802-4479
www.prudential.com

Along with Springsteen, Sinatra, and Bon Jovi, New Jersey can count Prudential Financial among its assets. Known mainly for its insurance business, the company has ramped up its investment management offerings via a steady diet of acquisitions. Prudential followed the 2003 acquisition of annuities distributor American Skandia with two deals in 2004—one for a South Korean asset management firm owned by Hyundai Investment & Securities; the other for Cigna's retirement business. At the end of the first quarter of 2006, it managed roughly $547 billion in assets. Its JennisonDryden mutual fund family was named the best-performing U.S. equity family of funds in the 2005 Lipper/Barron's Fund Families Survey.

The firm operates in three segments: Its Retirement segment offers retirement products and services, mainly to institutions; Asset Management, which had $169 billion in assets under management as of March 31, 2006, offers mutual funds and other investment products and services to institutions and individual investors. Finally, in 2003 it formed a brokerage joint venture with Wachovia, called Wachovia Securities, in which Prudential has a 38 percent stake.

The company didn't come through the scandal-ridden first part of the current decade completely unscathed. In 2004 it agreed to pay the NASD a $2 million fine to settle accusations of annuity fraud.

PUTNAM LLC

1 Post Office Square
Boston, MA 02109
Phone: 617-292-1000 or 800-225-1581
Fax: 617-482-3610
www.putnam.com

This old-school Boston mutual fund company has seen its reputation grow more tarnished than Paul Revere's original pewter mug, as a series of regulatory scandals have cast the firm and its parent in a less-than-responsible light. In 2003, the company became the first charged in the industry's mutual fund trading scandal and endured stories and accusations of certain shareholders skirting company policy by late-trading in fund shares.

Then, just as it was recovering from these allegations, New York State's attorney general levied charges of insurance bid-rigging against Putnam parent Marsh & McLennan.

Putnam has done its best to put the phrase "regulatory probe" behind it. It's made a $110 million settlement with the SEC and Massachusetts regulators, adopted reforms based on new mutual fund protection principles, replaced its CEO, shaken up the management of a number of its funds, and lowered the costs of owning a mutual fund. Nevertheless, while it was the number-four mutual fund company in 2000, by mid-2005 it was down to number nine. Assets under management fell 11 percent to $213 billion in 2004; as of the end of April 2006, they were down to $191 billion ($64 billion in institutional assets and $127 billion in mutual funds). Its institutional client roster is down to 177 clients from more than 250. It offers 78 mutual funds and has ten million shareholders and retirement plan participants. More than one industry observer has been heard to suggest that Marsh & McLennan might be smart to sell the company.

STATE STREET GLOBAL ADVISORS

1 Lincoln Street
Boston, MA 02111
Phone: 617-786-3000
Fax: 617-664-4299
www.statestreet.com

The sleeping giant of the asset management world, State Street Corp. quietly manages the most pension funds in the United States, while its trust and custody departments make it the top servicer of U.S. mutual and pension fund assets. Oh yeah, and its $1.5 trillion in assets under management make it the largest by that measure as well. The company has some 21,000 employees. State Street Global Advisors, its asset management arm, is primarily an institutional asset manager, investing in passive equity funds, active quantitative and fundamental equity funds, fixed-income, real estate, currency, and absolute return vehicles. The parent company, among other important roles, calculates most of the mutual fund prices that appear every day in the paper.

Although headquartered in Boston, State Street has offices in 26 countries. It's proud of being the first to launch an ETF with Standard & Poor's Depository Receipts in 1993. The firm recruits for investment support roles such as fund accountants, portfolio administrators, and tax claim coordinators.

TIAA-CREF

730 3rd Avenue

New York, NY 10017

Phone: 212-490-9000 or 800-842-2252

Fax: 212-916-4840

www.tiaa-cref.com

TIAA-CREF (the Teachers Insurance and Annuity Association–College Retirement Equities Fund) is one of the largest private pension managers around, keeping nest eggs warm for 3.2 million academics at 15,000 institutions. The company started in 1918 when the Teachers Insurance and Annuity Association was created with a $1 million endowment from the Carnegie Foundation. In 1952, the company created an annuity fund for investors, the College Retirement Equities Fund. The nonprofit offers savings products to the general public, but its typical customer tends to be in the academic, research, medical, or cultural sector.

In recent years, under the leadership of a former Merrill Lynch investment professional, Herb Allison, TIAA-CREF has adopted some of the practices of its for-profit brethren, trimming staff, streamlining its reporting structure, opening new offices to attract new clients and better serve existing ones, raising fund fees, and introducing new fund marketing fees. The company has been struggling with poor fund performance and the loss of business; in a big blow, it was recently fired by California's 529 plan due to poor performance and rising fees.

The company has 5,500 employees, and at the end of March 2006 had $380 billion in assets under management for 3.2 million retirement plan participants and 15,000 institutions. TIAA-CREF is also the largest institutional real estate investor in the United States. It has a reputation for being a progressive employer.

In 2005, Elizabeth Monrad left the company's CFO post after the launch of an investigation into whether she committed fraud at her former employer, General Re.

UBS GLOBAL ASSET MANAGEMENT

51 West 52nd Street
New York, NY 10019
Phone: 212-882-5000
Fax: 212-882-5892
www.ubs.com/e/globalam.html

UBS Global Asset Management was formed by the 1998 Swiss mega-merger of UBS and Swiss Bank Corp. Today, the firm is the second-largest mutual fund manager in Europe and the largest fund manager in Switzerland, and is making a name for itself as a leading shop for funds of hedge funds. It has offices in 30 countries, with main offices in London, Chicago, New York, Tokyo, and Zurich.

UBS Global Asset Management has a staff of more than 3,000, more than 600 of whom are investment professionals. A large number of clients in the United States have helped boost assets under management to $630 billion as of June 30, 2006, in no small part due to UBS's $12.5 billion acquisition of Paine Webber in 2000. (While UBS was happy about the significant increase in assets under management that came with PaineWebber, it hasn't been overjoyed with the acquisition; the PaineWebber business has performed relatively poorly since UBS acquired it.) The company offers traditional equity and fixed-income investments products, as well as alternative investments that include real estate and quantitative and hedge funds.

THE VANGUARD GROUP, INC.

100 Vanguard Boulevard
Malvern, PA 19355
Phone: 610-648-6000 or 800-662-7447
Fax: 610-669-6605
www.vanguard.com

Individual investor advocate John Bogle started Vanguard in 1975 in an effort to create low-cost funds. In keeping with the nautical theme of the company (the *Vanguard* was Admiral Horatio Nelson's first ship), Vanguard terms its 10,000 employees its "crew," the corporate cafeterias its "galleys," and so on. John Bogle's investment strategy has maintained Vanguard as a leader in low-management-fee funds. The company specializes in index funds (it claims to have created the first indexed mutual fund in 1976) and has grown to be the second-largest mutual fund company in the country as investors bet against their portfolio managers' ability to consistently beat the market. It also has quantitative funds that make portfolio decisions based on specific data-driven strategies. It believes that keeping the human element out of making investment decisions helps its funds avoid pitfalls like market mania. Like rival Fidelity, it's chipped away at the expense ratio on its largest indexes as one more way to pull in client assets.

Vanguard offers more than 130 domestic and 40 international funds, and has 21.5 million accounts, more than 12,000 of them in the U.S. Vanguard increased its assets under management by 10 percent in 2004 to more than $800 billion; as of April 30, 2006, the number had skyrocketed to $995 billion. In addition to ranking high in managed assets, Vanguard consistently gets accolades as an employer. The company prides itself on efforts to create an equal opportunity workplace, including diversity training for managers and diversity "councils" that focus on ways to make the workplace more equitable. Vanguard recruits at colleges in Pennsylvania, among other places.

WELLINGTON MANAGEMENT COMPANY, LLP

75 State Street
Boston, MA 02109
Phone: 617-951-5000
Fax: 617-951-5250
www.wellington.com

Though you've probably never heard of it, Wellington Management has been investing other people's money since 1928. The company has the distinction of offering the first balanced mutual fund, the Wellington Fund. It's also a leading subadvisor for other mutual fund companies, including Vanguard.

This Boston Brahmin has had a track record of slow but steady growth. It opened offices in San Francisco, Sydney, and Tokyo in 1997 and didn't open another until it hung out a shingle in Hong Kong in 2003. Worldwide, it has more than 1,000 clients. Along with its Boston headquarters, the firm has offices in Atlanta, Chicago, and Radnor, Pennsylvania.

The private partnership is an institutional asset manager, advising institutional clients and mutual fund sponsors in more than 40 countries. By March 2006, it was managing $542 billion in assets, some 68 percent of which were in equities. The company is known for its morning meeting, in which the investment management team, including senior executives, gathers to trade investment ideas.

The firm makes no bones about selecting future employees with the same care it takes in picking stocks. Advertisements for many of its positions reflect the company's search for experienced financial professionals, and its portfolio managers have an average 17 years of experience. More bluntly, it tells job seekers, "We're not right for everyone."

In 2005, the SEC announced that it was investigating the company over allegations that it allocated mutual fund shares improperly.

Largest Retail Brokerage Companies

The profiles of the biggest brokerages here appear in alphabetical order. This section includes retail brokerage as well as private banking operations. See the "Industry Rankings" section in the previous chapter for rankings by total client assets.

A.G. EDWARDS, INC.

1 North Jefferson Avenue
St. Louis, MO 63103
Phone: 314-955-3000 or 877-835-7877
Fax: 314-955-5547
www.agedwards.com

Considered a Main Street, rather than Wall Street, broker, A.G. Edwards plays off its Midwestern roots. Founded in 1887, it is one of the country's oldest full-service brokerage firms. It matches every client with one of its nearly 7,000 financial advisors in 700 offices nationwide and in Europe, who offer clients stocks, bonds, mutual funds, commodities, insurance, and mortgage products in a quota-free environment. The company also invests in private equity partnerships. A.G. Edwards has $343 billion in client assets.

Among the company's 15,480 employees are some 50 senior analysts, who cover more than 700 companies in more than 70 industries. In 2006, *Fortune* named A.G. Edwards one of the "Best Companies to Work For" for the 11th time. A.G. Edwards recruits recent graduates who have a bachelor's in finance and MBAs for investment analysis and investment banking positions. Thanks to the rising stock market, it hired 650 financial consultants in 2005, investing $75,000 to train each.

AMERIPRISE FINANCIAL, INC.

707 2nd Avenue South
Minneapolis, MN 55402
Phone: 612-671-3131 or 800-386-2042
www.ameriprise.com

Until recently, Ameriprise was one of three business segments of card and travel giant American Express Financial Corp. But in February 2005, AmEx announced plans to spin off the division, which was not performing at the same level as the rest of the company. The newly independent company provides financial planning, brokerage services, insurance, and other investments through a network of 12,000 financial advisors in 3,500 offices, as well as the Internet and other channels. It serves international clients via offices in London, Tokyo, and Singapore.

In 2005 it made $7.5 billion in net revenue, up 3 percent from 2004. As of the end of March 2006, Ameriprise was handling $264 billion in client assets. Like many others in the industry, Ameriprise has shelled out its share of regulatory fines, most recently in 2005, when it paid $24 million to settle charges of overcharging and steering customers improperly to in-house products. It's also been hurt by underperformance among the funds it manages.

Like seemingly everyone else in financial services these days, it's targeting the "mass affluent" market, those with more than $100,000 to invest.

BANC OF AMERICA INVESTMENT SERVICES, INC.

Gateway Village Building 900
900 West Trade Street
Charlotte, NC 28255
Phone: 800-926-1111
www.baisidirect.com

When Bank of America sealed its deal for FleetBoston in 2004, it inherited discount broker Quick & Reilly (and its 900,000 brokerage accounts), which it combined with its existing investment services business. Now the third-largest bank-owned brokerage and one of the biggest overall, BAI (as insiders call it) has $162 billion in total client assets as of March 31, 2006, up 14 percent from a year earlier. It provides online self-directed investing, with options for more active traders, plus investing via a personal financial advisor. BAI has more than 200 locations in 34 states.

BAI is part of Bank of America's Global Wealth & Investment Management business, which is a top-ten mutual fund manager and a top-five global money-market fund manager.

THE CHARLES SCHWAB CORPORATION

101 Montgomery Street
San Francisco, CA 94104
Phone: 415-636-7000 or 800-435-4000
Fax: 415-636-9820
www.schwab.com

Schwab revolutionized the brokerage industry in 1974 with its discount brokerage service, and it continued to add innovations through the dotcom era, becoming one of
the first brick-and-mortar companies to offer online trading. When the crash came,
however, Schwab was hit hard, and had to make several rounds of layoffs to bring oper-
ating expenses more in line with revenue. Indeed, the company had 26,300 employees
at the end of 2000, but just 14,000 at the end of 2005.

Schwab has moved up and along the food chain by offering "Signature" and private client services to high-net-worth customers, as it tries to replace trading commissions lost
when day traders returned to their day jobs. It bought wealth manager U.S. Trust and
also owns CyberTrader, a tech-rich online broker that targets serious, active traders. It
serves 6.7 million brokerage accounts, and handles $1.3 trillion in client assets.

Attempts to diversify its revenue beyond its retail core proved mostly unsuccessful. In
2004, less than a year after buying investment bank boutique Soundview Technology
Group, Schwab sold it. That venture, combined with lackluster revenue, prompted
Schwab's board to boot CEO David Pottruck and bring back founder Charles Schwab.
The firm, with some difficulty, has tried to carve out a spot between the no-frills discount brokers and the full-service firms. It's opened investor branches and has rolled
out an in-house equity selection service, even as it continues to cut rates on trades. In
2003, it launched a bank, Charles Schwab Bank.

For a firm founded on the idea of letting investors choose their own investments, Schwab has done pretty well in the advice department. Its equity model portfolio, which is based on its in-house stock-picking service, was ranked number one by *Barron's* for the 2000–05 period. Contrary to its late '90s image as a mostly Web broker, it hires quite a few warm bodies to reach out to clients: It recruits financial consultants with proven track records to staff its 3,300 offices. Compensation is based on revenue produced from the client's assets under management, and a financial consultant making $300,000 or more annually is not unheard of.

EDWARD D. JONES AND CO., LP

12555 Manchester Road
Des Peres, MO 63131
Phone: 314-515-2000
Fax: 314-515-2622
www.edwardjones.com

Your stock brokerage is named Edward, you're headquartered in Missouri—that narrows it down to two. Hardly a second fiddle to A.G. Edwards, the brokerage subsidiary of The Jones Financial Companies has carved out a special brokerage niche. Its new brokers build their business the old-fashioned way—walking door-to-door and sweet-talking local store owners and housewives. And it's eschewed such newfangled brokerage contraptions as Internet trading. There are nearly 9,000 Edward Jones offices, and the company handles $357 billion in client assets.

Despite its iconoclastic ways, Edward Jones has made strides where it counts. In 2006 it received the highest customer satisfaction rating among full-service brokerages from J.D. Power & Associates, for the second year in a row. Its 200 general partners and more than 5,000 associate partners own the firm, a growing rarity among the big brokerages; the partnership arrangement allows the firm to offer its brokers a liberal profit-sharing plan. Its squeaky-clean reputation was sullied in late 2004 when regulators accused Edward Jones brokers of guiding their customers to fund companies that, unbeknownst to the customer, were also paying the brokerage through an innocuous-sounding arrangement called "revenue sharing." It paid $75 million to settle the charges, and its top executive retired as a result (and paid $3 million of that $75 million).

Note, undergrads: Jones is also one of the few full-service brokerages that accepts greenhorns fresh out of college for its broker-training program. This, of course, encourages promotion from within. New brokers have defined goals that they must reach. They must make 25 real contacts a day and contact prospects at least once every two weeks before reaping the benefits of their own office with the Edward Jones name (as well as the broker's) on the door. That process usually takes 8 to 11 months.

E-TRADE FINANCIAL CORP.

134 East 57th Street
New York, NY 10022
Phone: 646-521-4300 or 800-387-2331
Fax: 212-826-2803
www.etrade.com

E-Trade Financial Corp., whose ticker symbol is the whimsical ET, has fought hard to keep afloat in the postbubble stock market. It's attempted to offset slowdowns in trading activity by pushing other financial products that the home investor might need. It tried to acquire Ameritrade in 2005, offering some $6 billion, but was rebuffed by the competitor, which preferred to stay independent.

In 2005, the company rolled out E-Trade Complete, an account that combines a customer's trading, investing, cash, and debt accounts. And it's made a number of acquisitions in recent years. The firm bought online broker Tradescape in 2002. Other recent acquisitions include Harrisdirect, the U.S. online broker, from the Bank of Montreal; investment manager Kobren Insight Management; and BrownCo, a broker for experienced online traders.

As of the end of 2005, it boasted some 3.6 million account holders, and handled $179 billion in client assets. E-Trade serves day traders via its E-Trade Professional Trading business.

Like many startups that survived the tech crash of 2000, E-Trade has shed much of its freewheeling dotcom identity (as well as a few employees—its 2005 headcount of 3,400, is 11 percent lower than its 2000 headcount of 3,800). It moved its headquarters to New York City from Silicon Valley, and the corporate culture is more suit than sandals these days. E-Trade has also been busy expanding overseas and now has online sites in nine countries outside the United States. The firm recruits from California and several East Coast universities.

FIDELITY PERSONAL INVESTMENTS

82 Devonshire Street
Boston, MA 02109
Phone: 617-563-7000
Fax: 617-476-6150
personal.fidelity.com

Already a pioneer in the mutual fund industry, Fidelity hooked its wagon to the discount brokerage star and has become one of the largest brokers in the country with more than 12 million brokerage accounts (as of March 31, 2006). Customers access Fidelity through the company's award-winning website, through its call centers, or by visiting its financial centers. Fidelity advisors offer not only Fidelity funds and its 401(k) rollover plans, but also popular funds of other firms, stocks, fixed-income investments, and asset management services.

Fidelity Investments also operates 110 investor centers across the United States. In addition to serving individual investors, it serves more than 3,000 registered investment advisors, as well as about 350 broker-dealers, with 70,000 brokers. Its online brokerage operation boasts $664 billion in client assets.

The company recently entered a strategic relationship with JPMorgan Chase, giving Fidelity clients access to deals lead-managed by that bank. It also recently entered into a partnership with Amazon.com to get information about its services in front of visitors to that site.

MERRILL LYNCH GLOBAL PRIVATE CLIENT

4 World Financial Center
250 Vesey Street
New York, NY 10080
Phone: 212-449-1000 or 800-637-7455
Fax: 212-449-9418
www.ml.com

Merrill Lynch is at or near the top in investment banking, institutional trading, and asset management. But perhaps the most impressive is its retail brokerage operation. Clients keep $1.5 trillion in assets at Merrill Lynch Global Private Client Group, making this the biggest brokerage operation. Global Private Client counts approximately 15,000 financial advisors in its ranks, who work out of some 600 offices around the world. "This is the bread and butter of Merrill," says one insider.

Indeed, the unit leaves few slices in the investing loaf untouched. Its online brokerage offers low-cost fixed-price trades. Customers with less than $250,000 in investable assets are advised by its financial advisory call center. With up to $1 million in assets, the customer gets a financial advisor. Wealth management advisors handle the up-to-$10 million crowd. And private banking and investment professionals take on the job of advising those who have $10 million or more socked away.

Global Private Client recruits undergrads and MBA candidates for its analyst and associate programs. These programs usually start the summer before your final year of school; Merrill makes offers for its two-year program based on summertime performance. Analysts typically work out of corporate campuses in Princeton, Hopewell, and Jersey City, New Jersey. Some get placed in the Big Apple. As an analyst or associate, you'll work in one of six areas that generally support Merrill's network of financial advisors: private banking and investment, retirement, investment and wealth management, direct services, marketing, and global banking. Support might mean helping create investment products or creating a marketing campaign. It doesn't mean selling bonds to Florida grannies, nor does it mean just running spreadsheet models. "We don't want individuals to sit [in] a cube all day and crunch numbers but to create a marketing campaign and analyze it, sell it," says an insider.

The company has seen its share of scandal in recent years. In 2002 it was fined $100 million for excessively bullish recommendations by its research department. More recently, in 2005, it paid $14 million to settle charges that it pushed clients into unnecessarily expensive mutual funds that paid brokers outsized commissions. Also in 2005, it paid $13.5 to the New York Stock Exchange for failing to supervise New Jersey brokers who were engaged in mutual funds market-timing improprieties.

MORGAN STANLEY

1585 Broadway
New York, NY 10036
Phone: 212-761-4000
Fax: 212-762-0575
www.morganstanley.com

Morgan Stanley's retail brokerage operations came to life via the 1997 merger between Dean Witter Discover, the dining card-cum retail brokerage, and white-shoe investment bank Morgan Stanley. Morgan Stanley dropped Dean Witter from its name in 2002, and its brokerage operations are now the among the largest in the country. Still, the Dean Witter acquisition has never really been considered successful, and in 2005, Morgan Stanley CEO Jack Purcell, who came to the company with Dean Witter, was forced out of his position.

Morgan Stanley offers a range of options to clients, with its focus on the high-net-worth customer. Morgan Stanley's individual investor group, which makes most of its money from commissions and asset management fees charged to its retail brokerage clients, had $633 billion in client assets at the end of February 2006, which was up just 2 percent from the previous year. The number of the group's registered representatives has slipped for the past four years; it now stands at 9,500.

RAYMOND JAMES FINANCIAL, INC.

880 Carillon Parkway
St. Petersburg, FL 33716
Phone: 727-567-1000 or 800-248-8863
Fax: 727-567-8915
www.rjf.com

From the sunny shores of Florida, Raymond James has spread its financial advisory services to 2,200 locations worldwide, including affiliates in Argentina and Turkey. It serves some 1.4 million brokerage accounts, and handles $150 billion in client assets. Raymond James has 4,800 financial advisors in the U.S. and another nearly 300 in Canada. Not surprisingly, the firm stresses that it's kept up-to-date with the latest technology for clearing and custody services.

Its slogan, "individual solutions from independent advisors," refers to its network of financial advisors, who can fall into one of five employment categories: traditional employee, independent employee, independent contractor, fee-only firm, and bank/credit union. Each of these models gives employees different levels of autonomy and has a different fee and payment structure. As an "independent employee," for instance, a financial advisor establishes his or her own branch office; Raymond James handles the human resources, payroll, technology and administrative support.

The company offers something called the Options rotational program for new undergraduate hires, which gives new employees a good overview of what the company does.

In September 2005, the firm was fined $7 million due to fraud perpetrated by one of its brokers.

SMITH BARNEY GLOBAL PRIVATE CLIENT GROUP

388 Greenwich Street
New York, NY 10013
Phone: 212-816-6000 or 800-EARNS-IT
Fax: 212-793-9086
www.smithbarney.com

With roots stretching back to the 19th century and a history packed with brokerage mergers, Smith Barney Private Client today claims more than 13,400 financial consultants and 600 offices, primarily in the U.S. It handles $1,130 billion in client assets in 7.1 million client accounts. The company is part of the financial services behemoth Citigroup.

In 2005, Citigroup swapped its asset management businesses for Legg Mason's brokerage operations. In the process, Smith Barney added more than 1,200 financial advisors and 124 branch locations in the mid-Atlantic and southeastern states.

Citi and Smith Barney have not been strangers to scandal in recent years. In 2003, Citi paid $400 million in fines for issuing overly bullish stock recommendations. In 2005, one of its brokers was indicted for allowing day traders to listen in on internal market analysis and other customers' trade orders. And as a result of not passing transfer agent discounts on to customers, the company has been forced to pay $208 million, and the SEC has charged a couple of former Citi executives with fraud.

Sister unit Smith Barney Equity Research recruits from the college crowd. But the brokerage looks for more experienced professionals when it comes to financial consultants. Applicants should have at least five years of business experience and a bachelor's degree. Successful candidates for the financial advisory program typically start in a 36-month paid training program.

TD AMERITRADE HOLDING CORPORATION

4211 South 102nd Street
Omaha, NE 68127
Phone: 402-331-7856 or 800-237-8692
Fax: 402-597-7789
www.tdameritrade.com

TD Ameritrade is the result of online brokerage pioneer Ameritrade's 2006 acquisition of the U.S. operations of TD Waterhouse, the brokerage arm of Canada's Toronto-Dominion Bank. By the end of the first quarter of 2006, the newly combined firm had $263 billion in client assets, and was serving six million accounts (3.3 million containing assets worth $2,000 or more). The acquisition also gave the company a brick-and-mortar presence of 140 offices in the U.S.

After the individual investing bonanza of the late 1990s shut down, Ameritrade made several acquisitions that picked up additional customers and assets. Among them: Datek in 2002, the assets of mydiscountbroker.com in 2003, and those of Bidwell & Co. in 2004. With trading activity still fragile, Ameritrade slashed fees for stock trades— as did its main rivals. Then came the TD Waterhouse acquisition.

Omaha-based TD Ameritrade also has an institutional client division. It continually launches new technical services and products designed to help traders manage their investments, and hopefully make more. Despite pressures facing all the online brokers, its service has won awards, including a four-star rating in *Barron*'s 2005 review of online brokers and the "Best Financial Services Customer Service" from J.D. Powers & Associates.

UBS WEALTH MANAGEMENT US

1285 Avenue of the Americas
New York, NY 10019
Phone: 212-713-2000
Fax: 212-713-9818
financialservicesinc.ubs.com

One of the largest banks in the world, UBS became a major force in retail brokerage when it purchased PaineWebber in 2000. Today, that investment is probably still not worth the $12.5 billion UBS paid for the firm at the time. That hasn't stopped UBS from shopping for other brokerage operations, though; in 2006, it announced plans to purchase the private client services arm of boutique investment banker Piper Jaffray, in a move that will add 800 financial advisors and 550 branch support personnel, in 90 retail offices in the Midwest and West, to its retail network.

In the United States, UBS helps individuals invest their money through its UBS Wealth Management broker/dealer. Prior to the Piper Jaffray acquisition, UBS had 7,500 registered financial representatives working out of more than 350 offices nation-wide, and handled $673 billion in client assets. UBS brokers spend much of their time calling on wealthy clients or taking the really wealthy ones out to lunch. Additionally, advisors are moving their customers to a fee-based, rather than transaction-based, model. That shouldn't be too hard for UBS's financial advisors, who receive nearly a year and a half of training to start.

UBS will accept brokers with a bachelor's degree; however, it prefers candidates with at least five years of work experience and really likes those with MBAs, JDs, or CFAs (Chartered Financial Analyst)—people who can command respect from potential investors. UBS offers a base salary to new advisors until they have completed the second stage of their training.

WACHOVIA SECURITIES, LLC

901 East Byrd Street
Richmond, VA 23219
Phone: 804-649-2311 or 800-999-4328
Fax: 804-782-3540
www.wachoviasec.com

Formed by the merger of the brokerage groups of Wachovia Bank (which owns 62 percent of Wachovia Securities) and Prudential Financial (which owns 38 percent), Wachovia Securities instantly became one of the country's largest retail brokerages when it was created in 2003; it's affiliated with the fifth-largest bank. Unlike its parent Wachovia Corp., the brokerage's 2,800 locations, more than 10,300 financial advisors, and 17,000 total employees are spread throughout the United States and in Argentina, Brazil, Chile, Paraguay, and Uruguay. It handles $684 billion in client assets, and serves 5.9 million retail client accounts, including 1.5 million online accounts.

Wachovia has been beefing up its brokerage staff in recent times. It hired 732 experienced brokers and 183 brokerage trainees in 2005, and is on track to hire similar numbers in 2006. "We're looking to build a more diverse brokerage unit," says one insider. That means it's looking for women and minorities, as well as young people in general, as it tries to deepen its talent pool.

Additional Asset Management Companies

Though the number of asset management companies and mutual fund advisors are legion, the following companies, though not the largest in the industry, are among the better known and offer ample opportunities for the job seeker.

AIM INVESTMENTS

11 Greenway Plaza, Suite 100
Houston, TX 77046
Phone: 713-626-1919 or 800-959-4246
Fax: 713-993-9890
www.aimfunds.com

Founded in 1976, AIM has strategically acquired its way to a global presence. It employs more than 1,593 people through its offices in Houston, Denver, Austin, and San Francisco. AIM manages 70 retail funds and 18 institutional funds, among other investment portfolios. A I M Distributors underwrites the funds, and the firm sells funds under the AIM and Invesco brands. AIM Investments is a subsidiary of Amvescap, a British company. The firm had $135 billion in assets under management as of June 30, 2006.

AMERICAN CENTURY INVESTMENT MANAGEMENT

4500 Main Street, Suite 1500
Kansas City, MO 64111
Phone: 816-531-5575 or 800-345-2021
Fax: 816-340-7962
www.americancentury.com

American Century Investment Management is a diversified family of funds. Started in 1958, it was one of the first to use a computer in portfolio management. Its more than 80 funds now range from conservative income to aggressive growth. The firm, which is part- owned by JPMorgan Chase, has roughly $95 billion under management.

American Century employs about 2,000 people and has offices in Kansas City; Leawood, Kansas; Denver; Mountain View, California; New York; and Singapore. The company has a reputation for having high ethical standards.

THE DREYFUS CORPORATION

200 Park Avenue
New York, NY 10166
Phone: 212-922-6000 or 888-271-4994
Fax: 212-922-7533
www.dreyfus.com

The Dreyfus Corporation, established in 1951, has been a subsidiary of Mellon Bank since 1994. Headquartered in New York City, Dreyfus manages more than $170 billion in assets in more than 200 mutual fund portfolios nationwide and is known for its Dreyfus Premier family of equity and bond funds. Originally a bond shop, Dreyfus can now claim to be more diversified; in recent times, nearly a third of its assets under management have been allocated to equity funds. It's also been selling more products through third parties such as financial planners than direct to the investors. In 2002, the company sold its online brokerage unit, Brown & Co., to JPMorgan Chase, and a year later, it bought Ashland Management.

GAMCO INVESTORS, INC.

1 Corporate Center
Rye, NY 10580
Phone: 914-921-5100 or 800-422-3554
Fax: 914-921-5392
www.gabelli.com

GAMCO (formerly Gabelli Asset Management) is known for its value-oriented style of investing. It manages mutual funds and offers separate accounts for high-net-worth individuals, institutions, and qualified pension plans, providing advisory services to approximately 30 funds and a couple thousand high-net-worth individuals. The company had $28 billion in assets under management as of the end of 2005, almost all of it in equities. Bill Gates owns a stake of GAMCO.

An acolyte of Warren Buffett, the king of value investing, the gregarious company founder Mario Gabelli believes in observing what's going on in society to help make investment decisions. He likes to hire PhDs because they're "poor, hungry, driven people."

JANUS CAPITAL GROUP INC.

151 Detroit Street
Denver, CO 80206
Phone: 303-333-3863
Fax: 303-336-7497
www.janusfunds.com

Janus Capital has seen turmoil in recent years. First, the publicly traded firm reorganized and merged with its parent company, Stillwell Financial, in 2003. Around that time, Janus admitted to engaging in market-timing activities. Add to that the tumultuous fate of technology stocks, in which Janus tended to have large positions, and you end up with a less-than-rosy predicament. In August 2004, it reached a $225 million final settlement with regulators over market-timing charges.

Janus had about $154 billion in assets under management as of March 31, 2006, a big drop from its peak of $258 billion in 2000. Besides its flagship Janus Capital Management, the firm owns institutional quantitative manager Intech and 30 percent of value investor Perkins, Wolf, McDonnell & Co. As it tries to put bad publicity behind it, Janus has tweaked its compensation structure for managers so that they're rewarded more for investment performance than growth in assets. Plus, new management has fleshed out analyst coverage so Janus' investments are decidedly less tech-heavy.

Janus has 1,465 employees.

LAZARD ASSET MANAGEMENT LLC

30 Rockefeller Plaza, 57th Floor
New York, NY 10112
Phone: 800-821-6474
www.lazardnet.com

One of the main divisions of 158-year-old European-American investment bank
Lazard, Lazard Asset Management invests assets for individuals and institutions in the
United States, Britain, Germany, Australia, and Japan, and serves as an advisor to several
mutual fund families. Under the direction of Wall Street dealmaker Bruce Wasserstein,
parent Lazard made its IPO debut in the spring of 2005—thus promising that a few of
the secretive institution's mysteries would make the light of day. As of March 31, 2006,
the company employed 640 financial advisory professionals, and had $94 billion in cli-
ent assets under management Lazard advises several mutual fund families.

NEUBERGER BERMAN INC.

605 Third Avenue
New York, NY 10158
Phone: 212-476-9000
Fax: 212-476-9090
www.nb.com

Since 1939, when the company was founded, Neuberger Berman has been striving to make the wealthy even wealthier. The company's namesake and founder, Roy Neuberger, was an art patron and investor who founded the company to cater to individuals like himself. The firm, which is now part of Lehman Brothers, manages more than 40 mutual funds for institutions and individuals and offers financial advisory services to both client segments. In keeping with its focus on the blue-blood set, it offers separate accounts for clients with $10 million in assets or more. Neuberger Berman has $116 billion in assets under management and employs 111 portfolio managers who have a combined average industry experience of 23 years.

OPPENHEIMERFUNDS, INC.

2 World Financial Center
225 Liberty Street
New York, NY 10281
Phone: 212-323-0200
Fax: 212-323-4070
www.oppenheimerfunds.com

A subsidiary of MassMutual, OppenheimerFunds—not to be confused with
Oppenheimer & Co.—has been in the investment management business since 1960.
Today, the company is one of the largest mutual fund companies in the United States,
offering more than 65 funds and managing $215 billion in client assets and six million
shareholder accounts as of March 31, 2006. The company has expanded its services to
include variable annuities and qualified retirement funds. It's also the parent of hedge
fund firm Tremont Capital Management.

T. ROWE PRICE GROUP, INC.

100 East Pratt Street
Baltimore, MD 21202
Phone: 410-345-2000
Fax: 410-345-2394
www.troweprice.com

Started in 1937, as of June 30, 2006, T. Rowe Price manages $294 billion in client assets for individuals, corporations, and institutions. Known for its growth style of investing, or finding companies whose earnings and dividends look like they'll grow faster than inflation and the overall economy, T. Rowe's fund performances have helped it reel in assets. Its Capital Appreciation Fund in 2005 was the only U.S. equity fund to post positive returns 15 years in a row, even through the most recent and quite severe bear market.

The Baltimore-based firm also has offices in Amsterdam, Buenos Aires, Copenhagen, Hong Kong, London, Paris, Singapore, and Tokyo.

On the Job

The Big Picture

Whether you're a "quant jock" who salivates like Pavlov's dog when you see a spreadsheet, or a social animal who jumps out of your seat to meet new people and build relationships, or even that rare beast who is both quantitative and social, the retail brokerage and asset management industries have fulfilling and lucrative opportunities to satisfy your yen.

Though many of the roles in the brokerage and asset management industries are similar, you can split these unsplittable industries in a few key ways. Asset management companies tend to have institutional investors and some wealthy individuals as customers, whereas retail brokerages primarily serve individuals. Roles in asset management companies are typically considered "buy-side"; that is, they are within companies that trade securities or analyze stocks for their own portfolios. Roles in the retail brokerage industry tend to be "sell-side," or within companies that trade or analyze stocks for clients that engage in trading.

Asset management companies, including hedge and mutual funds, are in the business of increasing the wealth of their constituent investors through the management of a pool of funds. Leading this endeavor is the fund manager, who executes the strategy of the fund and directs investments. Supporting the fund manager is a group of analysts. Analysts evaluate industries and the stocks and bonds issues within them. Bond analysts tend to be more technical and quantitative than stock analysts. Analysts often reside within a research group and work for multiple fund managers. Unlike analysts at securities firms, they also tend to evaluate stocks across industries. Also within the research department are a small number of economists and investment strategists who do very high-level strategy—they try to predict the direction of the economy and markets and come up with general portfolio strategies accordingly.

In addition, because they often deal in high volumes or very specialized securities, asset managers have in-house trading groups to manage the positions of a particular fund or group of funds. Asset managers also have a front-end team, a sales and relationship management team to find new investors, manage the accounts of existing investors, and, in the case of some direct-distribution mutual funds, market to the general public. Behind them is an array of support staff that includes financial analysts who do fund accounting, operations specialists who do trade settlement, compliance officers who ensure that employees are not engaging in insider trading or other illicit activities, and, in the case of mutual funds that deal directly with the public, customer service agents.

Retail brokerage firms tend to be slices of larger securities firms that also engage in institutional brokerage and investment banking. This guide focuses on roles within the retail portion of these companies. At the heart of retail brokerage firms are, astonishingly, brokers or financial advisors. Brokers not only execute securities trades for their clients and advise them on individual issues or mutual funds, they also help align their portfolios and in some cases, offer clients other financial products such as life insurance. Many retail brokerages have special departments for their wealthy clients, the financial services industry's equivalent of a casino's high-roller room. These private banking or private client services groups, as they are known in the industry, offer wealthy individuals attentive service and a number of nontraditional investment products. Private bankers are sort of the stockbrokers for the rich and famous. Supporting these brokers is a cast of characters similar to those in the asset management industry. Analysts provide recommendations on stocks for brokers to give to their clients; they also consult with a brokerage's traders to keep them informed of company developments that could trigger stock movements. The cast of characters is rounded out by compliance officers and operations, technology, and marketing groups.

You can find a large number of these positions outside of the massive asset management firms and brokerages. There are plenty of independent brokers and research firms. Most of these companies, however, are looking for people who have already earned their stripes in their respective departments of the major brokerage houses and asset management companies.

Finally, if you have spent time in the financial services industry and decide that you're yearning for a firm that makes something other than money, the finance departments at corporations usually welcome refugees from the finance industry with open arms. People making the jump back into corporate finance usually find the best fits as financial analysts and in investor relations.

Portfolio Management and Research Roles

FUND ACCOUNTANT

Salary: $35,000 to $50,000
Education: BA/BS in finance or accounting

As a fund accountant, you have a singular objective: To calculate the net asset value, the price that customers pay, for a mutual fund. You do this by tracking the fund's holding and closing prices for the securities owned as well as income earned and customer withdrawals. The job consists of checking ledger entries, running valuation reports, and recording account transactions.

An accounting or finance degree is a typical requirement. In some firms, the position is seen as a way of learning about the fund industry and portfolio management.

JUNIOR RESEARCH ANALYST

Salary: $60,000 to $100,000
Education: BA/BS

Typically an entry-level position at a firm such as Goldman or Merrill, this prized role does the bidding of the equity analyst. The role includes reading 10-Ks to find new company information, updating and maintaining financial models, synthesizing and analyzing external company and industry data, proofreading PowerPoint presentations and research reports, conducting primary research by calling industry contacts, and writing minor research reports and analyst notes. The role is essentially the assistant to an analyst or group of analysts. However, it brings you incredible exposure within the company and sets you up in an analyst track. Most junior analysts get MBAs and continue in the industry as associates, then senior analysts, and eventually managing director. Junior analyst roles are entry-level or require one to two years of experience.

Many firms look for people with accounting or finance degrees. However, top firms such as Credit Suisse will take college graduates from a wide range of majors, as long as they have excellent quantitative and communications skills.

ECONOMIST

Salary: $65,000 to $150,000
Education: BA/BS, MS/MA, PhD

Are you a budding Alan Greenspan, who wants a piece of the action now? Economists sit in both buy-side and sell-side companies. As an economist, you typically provide an opinion on the future of the market and general economy based on models that you develop and maintain, third-party models and analysis, and analysis of global and domestic news and economic indicators. You communicate your position on the economy and the market through written analysis briefs and meetings with internal clients—analysts and portfolio managers.

QUANTITATIVE ANALYST

Salary: $100,000-plus
Education: MS, PhD

Black hole physics got you down? Tired of trying to make cocktail party conversation with your game theory dissertation and bringing home dates to your shared apartment with milk-crate bookshelves? If there was ever a place for physics and math PhDs to become as rich as Croesus, it's as a quantitative analyst.

Quantitative analysts typically develop computer models to value securities and structure portfolios that are used in portfolio management and program trading. The position usually requires programming skills such as C or Java in addition to superior analytical skills and good communication skills—you have to meet with clients as well. Prospective candidates usually don't have to have previous finance experience for this position—firms will train you in portfolio theory, valuation, and securities regulation. They'll assume you'll be a quick study; though you aren't necessarily an Einstein, you are very likely a rocket scientist.

BUY-SIDE RESEARCH ANALYST

Salary: $150,000 to $1 million (for the big Wall Street firms)
Education: BA/BS, MBA
Credential: CFA (Chartered Financial Analyst)

Fixed-income analysts typically work in small teams of up to a dozen analysts, and perform credit analyses of individual securities and analyses of the overall market. Analysts usually support a portfolio manager but report to a director within the research department. The analyst's product is a recommendation to a fund manager to buy, sell, or hold a security. Additionally, analysts come up with investing ideas for portfolio managers based on their research. Analysts spend most of their time analyzing the cash flows of the companies underlying the securities they are evaluating, researching economic and social trends to understand the direction of interest rates, talking to analysts at credit rating agencies such as Moody's (for fixed-income securities) or to sell-side analysts at brokerage firms to better understand the securities and the market, and presenting their recommendations and findings to fund managers.

The role typically requires an MBA in finance, work toward a CFA, and significant quantitative abilities.

SELL-SIDE RESEARCH ANALYST

Salary: $150,000 to $1 million-plus
Education: BA/BS, MBA
Credential: CFA

Research analysts are a little like real-life doctors who play doctors on television; they have all the skills, training, and experience required of their profession and, on top of that, they have a public presence and communication skills that would put Dale Carnegie to shame. Brokerage firms put their analysts in the spotlight, helping them get spots on CNBC or *MoneyTalk*; their reputation adds luster and brand recognition to the firm. Not all analysts are this high-profile, but all must do their share of media snippets and conferences. The equity research position is not a role for the shy or the tongue-tied. Research analysts evaluate equities in a given industry, as well as the industry itself. With the financial models they develop, and through data they collect from 10-Ks, analyst calls, meetings with industry executives, and general industry knowledge, research analysts recommend (or pan) stocks and give opinions about where they think the industry is headed; they do this for both internal and external clients.

It's important to note that research teams are generally cost centers in brokerages. They don't generate revenue on their own, but rather support investment bankers and traders by giving them briefings on equities; in the past, they also touted stocks of investment banking clients to goose I-banking sales.

PORTFOLIO MANAGER

Salary: $200,000 to $1 million-plus
Education: BA/BS, often MBA
Credentials: CFA

The previous rung on the career ladder for most portfolio managers is investment or research analyst, or possibly junior portfolio manager. After passing on your stock picking analysis to the bloke running the fund, you have the chance to make your own calls. As a portfolio manager you're at the pinnacle of the asset management world. At some level, the job is pretty straightforward: Your company, be it a mutual fund, pension fund, or other fund, has specific investment goals, and your job is to pick a portfolio of stocks, bonds, or combination of the two, to make the highest returns for investors given those goals. The job is analytical, strategic, and on some level, sales-oriented.

All of the following might be part of a day: You order traders to execute the purchase or sale of securities. You meet with the CEO of a company you're thinking of investing in to grill him about the business. You huddle with your assistant manager or analysts to go over stock picks, optimization of short-term instruments like money market securities, and your fund's alpha rating. You then work with them to tweak the financial model that's the basis of your day-to-day fund management. You spend some time getting briefed on industry developments and corporate intelligence. Add to that client-relations work. If you are managing a pension or other asset fund, you might make a sales call to brief a charitable foundation on your investing strategy or meet with the investment manager of a current client to review your fund's performance.

Broker/Advisor Roles

Retail brokerage and financial advisory are, ultimately, sales jobs. Although you advise people on the best way to invest their wealth, you're in the business of getting them to buy your financial services and/or related products, be they stock transactions, life insurance, mutual funds, or portfolio planning. It's important to know this when considering the profession—to be successful you need to be a good salesperson, networking, building trust, and getting sales. In the institutional world, you are still making sales, but your clients are brokerage firms or banks that you are trying to persuade to carry your fund, institutions whose money you are trying to invest, or corporations whose assets you are trying to manage.

STOCKBROKER ASSISTANT

Salary: $30,000 to $50,000
Credentials: Series 7, 63

A stockbroker assistant performs many of the administrative tasks for a stockbroker, such as calling clients to confirm trades, attending to client requests, and handling reporting. After you've secured your Series 7 license, you become actively engaged in explaining products to clients, opening new accounts, and eventually executing trades. In a good firm, the broker assistant position represents an excellent way to become licensed and learn the business.

STOCKBROKER/FINANCIAL ADVISOR

Salary: $75,000 to $1 million-plus
Education: BA/BS; MBA, JD, or MD preferred
Credentials: Series 7, 63

Your job is to acquire new clients, then sell them a variety of products, from stock recommendations and mutual funds, to annuity-based life insurance. In the world of wealth management, you're getting people who are hardworking and smart enough to stock up hundreds of thousands or even millions of dollars to entrust you with their life savings.

Accordingly, many brokerage firms aren't looking for inexperienced kids to fill the ranks of the financial advisory and stock brokerage practices. Typically, firms recruit people with significant life experience and professional accomplishments. Merrill Lynch, for instance, looks for people with at least five years of professional experience and preferably with a professional degree such as an MD or JD. Other firms, such as Edward Jones, hire undergraduates. Most brokerages give their financial advisors significant training. In addition to Series 7 (the license required to sell securities) training, firms give up to five years of ongoing training in stock market basics, investment planning, asset allocation, and sales.

Compensation structures vary greatly among firms in the industry, but incentive-based pay is typical. Charles Schwab pays based on revenue produced by the broker's client assets under management, and making more than $150,000 a year is not unrealistic. Edward Jones pays entirely on commission after a year of training and ramp-up. Most firms will pay you a base salary until you build up a clientele, after which your salary is often entirely commission based.

Stock brokering is not for the faint of heart. In addition to offering income that's based solely on your performance and spiced by overall economic conditions, it's grueling until you build up your client base. Piper Jaffray expects that for the first three to five years, 50- to 60-hour workweeks are the norm. And you have to be ready for rejection. One insider reports the following statistics in prospecting for clients: "You might make 100 calls to clients. Of those calls you might actually get to leave a message or talk to someone 25 percent of the time. From there, you might get a callback from or talk to 15 people. Of those, you might schedule two or three initial advisory sessions—prospects."

Just like any other sales job, you have to do a lot of cold-calling and play the numbers game when you are starting out. And you have to have pretty thick skin. When you're starting out, you might be making 100 to 150 calls a day. An insider says, "It can get pretty discouraging. I make a plan for myself: I make perhaps 15 or 20 calls. I get called all sorts of names by some people; it can get brutal. I then walk away and do something else for a half hour and start up again."

INSTITUTIONAL RELATIONSHIP MANAGER

Salary: $100,000 to $175,000
Education: BA/BS, MBA
Credential: Series 7, 63

Relationship managers ensure that institutional clients of mutual funds or other institutional products are happy; they resolve issues, educate clients on products, and implement new processes. Relationship managers also advise and sell clients new products. Typically, relationship managers deal with large institutions and do so at a senior executive level. Usually, this is a midcareer position.

INSTITUTIONAL SALES MANAGER

Salary: $150,000 to $500,000
Education: BA/BS, MBA
Credential: Series 7, 63

Sales managers call on pension funds, union plans, banks, and other institutional clients and sell them funds, back-office products, or other products. They usually operate on a territory model, prospecting for new clients and selling add-on products to existing customers in a specified geography. The job involves some travel, sometimes up to 50 percent, which is high for the financial services industry. It also involves some cold-calling and a lot of networking, particularly with the fund consultants who act as a middle-man between the pension plans and companies that manage funds. Some firms expect sales reps to generate up to 20 warm leads (in-person presentations) a month. Often, sales managers have telesales staffs to help prospect for new clients. Once at a client presentation, you'll pitch your fund with a product team. It's also a midcareer hire. Those with aspirations in this potentially very lucrative business often start as traders or analysts, since knowing the industry backward and forward is key.

PRIVATE BANKER/PRIVATE CLIENT SERVICES

Salary: $150,000 to $1 million-plus
Education: MBA
Credentials: Series 7, 63

Private bankers are like financial advisors on steroids. They offer financial services and advice to wealthy individuals and earn wads of cash for their efforts. Their profiles can range from a bank-branch employee schooled in products that might interest people with assets of more than $250,000 in investing, to brokerage wealth managers catering to families with more than $500 million in assets. These bankers are often highly specialized and carry multiple degrees. Private banking units usually charge their clients a fee for their services based on a percentage of assets under management. So the more assets a client brings to the institution, the sweeter the payout to the banker, who receives a percentage of these fees over time for her hard work.

As with any financial advisory, private bankers have to build their own clientele, and a wealthy one at that. Private client-services brokers often find themselves living the jet-set life of their clients. One insider reports having to take his client to the Masters tournament in Augusta and later meeting another client, a casino entrepreneur, in Las Vegas.

And like mere financial advisors, private bankers typically have at least five years of professional experience as well as professional degrees such as MDs and JDs. A law degree is particularly attractive further up the wealth ladder, since understanding legal-ese comes in handy when helping clients in areas like estate planning. Aside from hiring well-connected people, private banks recruit relatively heavily from MBA programs. Although you still need to be connected, MBA recruiting affords an entrée into private client services that you might not otherwise have had.

This story illustrates two things: First, to be successful in private banking, you need to have a Rolodex with a few impressive names, or at least be only a degree or two of separation from them. Second, you have to be able to gain the trust of people who are not only fabulously wealthy, but among the most powerful individuals in their fields. It's not a business for the meek or for the isolated.

 WHEN PETER MET LEXI

As an undergrad at Columbia University, Peter Bacanovic met Alexis Stewart. Through Alexis he also met her mother Martha. Fast-forward a few years. When he became a stock-broker at Merrill Lynch, Pierce, Fenner & Smith, Peter Bacanovic no doubt told Martha about his new job and how he might be able to help her. Martha took him up on the offer—after all, she had known him for years.

Support Roles

CUSTOMER SERVICE

Salary: $25,000 to $45,000
Education: BA/BS

If you're determined to get into the asset management or brokerage industries and all else fails, you could look for a position in a customer service department. Here, you help customers understand their transactions, read their statements, and sort through product information. The role gives you a grounding in the industry and the company. Customer service agents typically need Series 7 and 63 licenses, which firms will often sponsor.

COMPLIANCE OFFICER

Salary: $40,000 to $150,000
Education: BA/BS

Compliance groups police securities and investment firms to prevent company employees from violating SEC regulations. Roles in compliance usually start at the analyst level and move up to vice president. Compliance officers set up "Chinese walls," or barriers between different groups in the company to prevent the spread of insider trading; monitor communications to prevent insider information from spreading outside the firm or between groups; track employees trades to ensure that they aren't buying or selling "gray list" securities; work with different company groups to establish gray lists or lists of clients that the firm is working with and on which the firm may have insider information; and develop the policies and procedures of the group along with company attorneys and external regulators.

Real People Profiles

MUTUAL FUND PORTFOLIO MANAGER

Years in business: seven
Age: 38
Education: BA in history, MBA
Hours per week: 50 to 55
Size of company: 500 employees
Certification: not required
Annual salary: more than $200,000

What do you do?

I manage a stock fund whose exclusive investor is a large pension fund; it's not for mom-and-pop investors. My fund specializes in telecommunications stocks. I pick the stocks we buy and sell, and it's my job to be familiar with the industry as a whole, analyze particular companies, and meet with the management of the companies we invest in. I do a lot of modeling and projections, but I also have to do some marketing and press relations.

How did you get your job?

I got my job by working in the industry for a while and getting to know lots of people. I got my first mutual fund job through the career center at Stanford, where I got my MBA. After several years in the industry, I'd made a lot of connections, and I got head-hunted for my current position.

What are your career aspirations?

Ten years from now, I want to be doing something very similar to what I'm doing now: managing money, researching new companies, and so on. The excitement of working in mutual funds is not in changing jobs, but staying abreast of the changes in the markets and the economy generally.

What kinds of people do really well at this business?

People who think in webs do well at picking stocks. You have to be intellectually curious, and you have to be able to synthesize ideas. If you know A equals B, and B equals C, then you have to figure out that A equals C, too. You have to be able to make connections, but the connections aren't always obvious.

What do you really like about your job?

My job is like a window on the world. To be good, you have to keep up with a constantly changing world. In the telecommunications industry, there's always a whole new set of companies to learn about. And the stock market is like a daily jolt of adrenaline, whether it goes up or down.

What do you dislike?

I live on the West Coast, so I have to get up really early if I want to follow the markets in New York. Also, you're bound to make mistakes—pick the wrong stocks—and it can be painful when you're wrong, even if you learn something in the process. This business is humbling.

What is the biggest misconception about this job?

People often don't understand what I do. People who don't know finance think it's like being a banker. They don't understand the rapidity of the changes a mutual fund manager deals with. Basically, they don't understand how exciting it can be.

How can someone get a job like yours?

An MBA is the most useful route to becoming a fund manager. People should also be willing to take a job beneath their talents when they start out. If you show good judgment, you can advance rapidly, so be willing to take whatever offer comes your way. You've also got to be willing to relocate to a big city.

Describe a typical day.

7:00 a.m.   Have to get in early so I can watch the market. Get to my desk, skim *The Wall Street Journal*, and check my email and voicemail. In particular, I want to check to make sure transactions from the previous day were completed.

8:00 a.m.   Attend a regular meeting with other portfolio managers for a general discussion of the market, plus discussion of specific stocks. People recommend specific articles in *The Wall Street Journal*, that kind of thing.

9:15 a.m.   Start reading the mass of information on my desk. I'm a slow reader, but I know how to skim for the necessary information quickly.

10:30 a.m.   Place phone calls to management of several different companies we're thinking of investing in to fill in gaps in our research and get more of a feel for the companies.

11:30 a.m.   Call securities analysts at a couple of brokerage firms to pick their brains about certain stocks.

12:00 p.m.   Lunch at my desk.

12:30 p.m.   Prepare for a meeting with management from a company we're thinking of investing in. Look over their numbers and prepare questions.

1:00 p.m.   Meet with representatives from the company. They make a brief presentation introducing the company, and then I ask questions about financial ratios, future plans, and overall competitive strategy.

2:00 p.m.   Talk informally with some of the people I manage, including analysts and researchers. We talk about various stocks. I ask their opinions on some companies I'm studying.

2:30 p.m.   Prepare for a meeting with another company we're thinking of investing in.

3:00 p.m.   The meeting proceeds very much like the previous one.

4:00 p.m.   Have to make a marketing call to a huge potential investor explaining the investment goals of our fund.

4:30 p.m.   Go back to my reading, which includes company press releases, IPO documents, our own analyses, and analyses from the sell side (i.e., brokerage houses). Meanwhile, check to see how the market has performed, especially the stocks we own.

6:30 p.m.   Call it a day.

MUTUAL FUND INVESTMENT ANALYST

Years in business: four

Age: 33

Education: BA, MBA

Hours per week: 50 to 60

Size of company: 2,000 employees

Certification: Chartered Financial Analyst

Annual salary: $250,000

What do you do?

As an analyst, I cover the business services and transportation industries. I also co-manage a midcap stock fund, which specializes in companies worth between $1 billion and $8 billion. I do financial modeling, meet with company management, and in general perform strategic assessments of both companies and industries. As a portfolio manager, I also make decisions about asset allocation—exactly how much money we're going to invest and where.

How did you get your job?

I got my job through on-campus recruiting at UCLA's business school. A UCLA alum who manages a fund at my firm placed the ad. I probably stood out because I had experience in business valuation; I'd done M&A-type work with Peat Marwick (now part of KPMG) and Merrill Lynch. I was also singularly focused on getting into the industry. Being an interviewer myself, I can tell who really wants to get into the industry.

What are your career aspirations?

Basically, I want to be doing what I'm doing now. Hopefully, I'll be managing a larger fund, perhaps one with $500 million or $1 billion in assets. I'm definitely interested in growth as opposed to value investing, so I'd like that to be my focus.

What kinds of people do really well at this business?

You should have a driving curiosity. You should have the instincts of a detective—the desire to turn over every stone so you can find out information that other people might not have. You also have to be a self-starter. Your only deliverable is your own opinions, so it's up to you to form them.

What do you really like about your job?

There's huge independence with this work. Plus, you have a lot of high-level contacts. I met with the CEO of Starbucks today, for example. I also like the focus on strategy. There's no right answer, so you pit your best guess against that of others. You have the potential to earn lots of money, and you're surrounded by people with lots of brainpower.

What do you dislike?

Sometimes there's less human interaction than I'd like. You spend a lot of time poring over numbers: SEC documents and company reports. And of course like everywhere, there are company politics. But I'd say they're both minor points overall.

What is the biggest misconception about this job?

You're not just crunching numbers, which is what most people think. There's a lot of strategizing, and that requires personal assessment of companies and industries. You make lots of qualitative assessments, too, assessing not just sales and profits but also management styles, for example.

How can someone get a job like yours?

First of all, you should be literate with numbers. You also have to demonstrate that driving curiosity. There are very few positions, so candidates who know the industry well are definitely going to stand out. Do the research. You might also consider getting a CFA [Chartered Financial Analyst] certificate. It'll show you're serious about the industry.

Describe a typical day.

7:00 a.m. As soon as I get in, check quotes for the previous day's biggest gainers and losers, just to make sure there are no disasters. Then I read *The Wall Street Journal* and scan for any stories about companies we're invested in. Then I listen to about 15 voicemails from brokers who may have tips or other trade information to convey.

9:00 a.m. Head to our daily departmental meeting. Basically, we just swap ideas, share major news items—that kind of thing. People throw out their daily tidbits.

9:30 a.m. Have to prepare for a lunch meeting with a company we're considering investing in. Pore over annual reports, SEC documents, and other data and analyses.

11:30 a.m. The company's representatives arrive and start their "road show," which is basically them pitching their company to us. They're trying to convince us they're a good investment. Lunch is served, so we're eating and taking notes at the same time. It's kind of like being in school, except we're not just students but also judge and jury.

1:30 p.m. Head back to my office and write down some thoughts about the company. Basically, I have to decide whether it's a worthwhile investment and then make my recommendation. So it takes some time and thought.

3:00 p.m. Consult with a sell-side analyst at Merrill Lynch. We compare notes on a couple of companies we're both studying. Since they're on the sales side, they're generous with their research in the hopes of generating a sale.

4:00 p.m. Take an hour to talk with a few executives at another company we're considering investing in. They're opening a new division, and I want to find out what their plan is and how it fits with their overall company strategy.

5:00 p.m. Spend the last part of my day doing research on a number of different companies. Fine-tune some financial models I've been working on, and then go over some models from the sell side to make sure they jibe with our own analyses.

6:30 p.m. Done for the day. Head to the gym.

RETAIL BROKER

Years in business: nine

Age: 37

Education: BS in civil engineering

Hours per week: more than 40

Size of company: 7,000 consultants nationally, 5 in my local branch, with a staff of 40

Certification: none

Annual salary: $250,000 to $300,000

What do you do?

In a nutshell, I help retirees and pre-retirees manage their money. I find out what's important to them financially and help them set objectives. I do a lot of analysis and then I put together a five- or six-page document, which lays out the big picture for a client. Once we have a plan, I'll talk to and meet with my clients on a regular basis. I personally review and analyze their portfolios. I'm currently working on a combination of commissions and fees, but will probably be moving toward all fees soon.

How did you get your job?

My mother was the wire operator in the office, and I got to know the people there while I was in high school and college. After a six-year stint in the Navy, I was offered a job working under a consultant/broker in the office. I trained and worked on my own for about six months, then my predecessor retired and gave me his book of clients, which amounted to about two-thirds of my assets at the time. I continued to build my business from there.

What are your career aspirations?

I hope to be doing exactly this for the rest of my career, with a few refinements. I would like my client list to include only clients I really like and whose business I want.

I would like to be able to engineer my time so that I spend most of it doing the activities I enjoy the most, such as meeting with clients and making presentations. And I would like to be supported by a staff who can take care of all the other stuff and who enjoy their part in the process as much as I enjoy mine. Ultimately, I hope to build my business to where I am generating $10 million a year in recurring revenue.

What kinds of people do really well at this business?

You should not be overly analytical, which can lead to "CFP" syndrome—for "can't friggin' produce." If you're an investment genius but [you] have no people skills, you're better off as an analyst. You should be outgoing and personable. Introverts just won't cut it. And you should have a solid work ethic. The first years building a client base can require 70- to 80-hour weeks, and you will have to take anything you can get until you become more established.

What do you really like about your job?

Of course I like the compensation. And I like the exposure I get to all different kinds of great people. I really feel I get to add value to their lives, and I don't just mean financially. I get to know people well and become their grief counselor, their marriage counselor—they'll even come to me for a recommendation on a new car.

What do you dislike?

The worst part is that there's a lot of minutiae, and it's getting worse. Every time some jerk does something to try to rip someone off, another regulation comes about, and we spend a lot of time complying with that stuff. I'm trying to train my staff to take care of more of that.

What is the biggest misconception about this job?

That it's easy money. There is no shortcut. You have to put in a lot of hours and a lot of hard work, especially in the beginning.

How can someone get a job like yours?

You could try to assume my identity and have me assassinated. Other than that, having a military background is seen as good because you get used to working long hours for horrendous pay. You definitely need some kind of work experience, preferably in sales. And you at least need the technical skills required to pass the Series 7, which is fairly mathematical.

Describe a typical day.

7:00 a.m.   Two days a week are set aside for meetings with clients, making presentations, and generating new contacts. The other days are where I get the office work done. On those days, I spend the first half-hour or so getting oriented. I'll drink coffee (although I'm trying to be good and drink more water), check my email, and mentally prepare for what I need to do that day.

7:30 a.m.   Talk with my assistant about some regulatory forms that need to be attended to. There seem to be more and more of these things every day.

8:00 a.m.   Start looking through some client portfolios to evaluate how everything's working. I can spend most of a morning or an entire day doing this.

10:30 a.m.   My review process is interrupted by a phone call from a client who has a question about a particular investment idea. I tell him I'll look into it and get back to him.

11:00 a.m.   Have a staff training meeting scheduled, something I've been doing more and more of these days.

12:30 p.m.   Meet with one of my clients for lunch. Since many of my clients are retirees, they're usually pretty available for lunches.

1:45 p.m.   Back at the office, I review some of the numbers my assistant has dug up regarding the investment idea my client wanted checked. Look them over and call the client with my opinion. Tell him I think it's a little risky in this market and advise that we stay away from it.

2:15 p.m.   Resume looking at client portfolios and make some notes about things to change and people to call.

3:00 p.m.   Put the finishing touches on a presentation I'll be making to a new client the following day. He's about to retire in a year and has lost a lot of money in his 401(k) due to the downturn. He's not in desperate straits, but I'd like to see his money somewhere much safer.

3:30 p.m.   Head home and mentally prepare for the coming day, which will be full of face-to-face time—the part of the job I like best.

The Workplace

Lifestyle, Hours, and Culture

Workplace Diversity

Travel

Compensation

Vacation, Benefits, and Perks

Career Path

Insider Scoop

Lifestyle, Hours, and Culture

If you're not one of those fortunate enough to have your trust fund managed by a premium asset manager or retail brokerage, the next best thing is to work in the retail brokerage or asset management industry. Though the work is demanding and the hours can be long, especially starting out, insiders are happy to roll in piles of money all day (even if it's someone else's). Aside from very attractive compensation, the industry promises (usually) manageable hours, good vacation, benefits unrivalled by nearly any industry outside of the public sector, and ample challenges.

But you don't have to take our word for it. According to *Fortune* magazine, the asset management and retail brokerage industries are pretty good places to work. Seven of *Fortune*'s "100 Best Companies to Work For" in 2006 are asset managers or retail brokers in one way or another, the same number as in 2005 and 2004.

Best Brokerage and Asset Management Firms to Work For

Rank	Company	Industry
16	Edward Jones	Retail brokerage
22	American Century Investments	Asset management
31	Robert W. Baird	Retail brokerage
37	American Express	Retail brokerage
60	Vanguard Group	Mutual fund management
63	Russell Investment Group	Asset management
70	A.G. Edwards	Retail brokerage

Note: Rankings reflect position in *Fortune*'s list.
Source: "100 Best Companies to Work For," *Fortune*, January 24, 2005

If investment banking hours are insane, most investment management jobs are merely crazy. In the make-or-break first few years, you can expect to work 50- to 60-hour weeks or more, and those hours will be action-packed. You will probably never have breakfast, lunch, or dinner alone again. There are meetings of every kind where you'll keep in touch with the movers and shakers of a particular industry. If you're in retail, there are hundreds of calls to make, clients to schmooze, parties to throw, and hours of research to be done.

As a broker or asset manager, you can expect to be given a high degree of independence in how you spend your time. The flip side is that the weight of building a client base of a winning portfolio falls directly on your shoulders. This means you should be entre-preneurial by nature and able to work creatively in your approach to acquiring clients or beating the S&P 500. If you go into retail brokerage, within two or three years you'll usually have no salary and be working entirely for commissions or fees. But if this kind of pressure excites and motivates you, this could be a great career choice.

As is often the case when money plays a major role, the industry tends to be on the conservative side. While not as staid as investment banking, the culture of asset manage-ment and brokerage professionals is relatively formal, especially in client-facing roles. And the higher up the corporate ladder you climb, the more likely it is that you'll be expected to wear a suit every day—a sharp one and, particularly if you're on the East Coast, a black or navy blue one at that. Dress codes and the culture in general tend to loosen up as you move west, especially if you end up in California. The industry is an odd mix of hierarchy and meritocracy, say insiders. But, as always, money talks. And nothing earns respect quite like being a big producer.

Workplace Diversity

The securities industry in general is still dominated by white men, particularly at higher levels of management. A 2003 survey by the Securities Industry Association found that 79 percent of executive managers at surveyed firms were white men, compared to 15 percent white women, 4 percent men of color, and 2 percent women of color. The biggest showing for women was in lower-level positions: They made up three-fourths of brokers' assistants. For minorities, representation was pretty slim across the board.

That said, women and minorities have made a lot of progress at certain firms. At Edward Jones, for example, 65 percent of staff are women. At Vanguard, women make up 45 percent of staff, and minorities make up 21 percent. Meanwhile, at much smaller asset manager American Century, some 49 percent of staff are women. The 2006 *Working Mother* "Best Companies for Women of Color" list included American Express and JPMorgan Chase, and the most recent *Working Mother* list of the best companies for women included American Express, Bank of America, Citigroup, Credit Suisse, Deutsche Bank, JPMorgan Chase, Lehman Brothers, MetLife, Morgan Stanley, Northern Trust, Prudential Financial, UBS, and Wachovia.

Important to the rising class of young bankers and brokers: There are several executives at the top of the biggest firms who don't fall into the "old white boy" category. Witness Sallie Krawcheck, who was previously CEO of Smith Barney and in 2004 became Citigroup's CFO. Stan O'Neal, chairman and CEO of Merrill Lynch, is one of the most powerful African-Americans in corporate America. Though the situation is far from perfect, the financial services industry seems intent on promoting talent regardless of color or gender. Indeed, half of Merrill Lynch Global Private Client Group's analyst program is typically made up of women. Success in the industry can be measured in concrete terms; if you make money for your company, it's hard to prevent you from getting ahead. The industry also has a reputation for fast-tracking stars. The trip from analyst to managing director can be made in a little more than ten years—so fasten your seatbelt.

Travel

The extent of travel will depend on your area of expertise in a company. If you're a marketing manager with a company that's opening additional branches or investment centers, you can bet that you'll be on the road most of the time, with long layovers (could be weeks or months) in cities where new openings require splashy promotions. Likewise, if you're a relationship manager or salesperson for a mutual fund or asset management company, you may spend a fair amount of time traveling across the country to see your clients.

For the most part though, travel in the industry is minimal. If you're working the phones, talking to investors on a daily basis, or performing analysis, you're going to be mostly office-based, with only an occasional trip for extra training or an incentive vacation. Portfolio managers take short trips to meet company CEOs and get ground-level information on the companies they invest in. And consider this: As a portfolio manager looking at prospective investments, the CEOs are trying to impress you, which makes the travel much more enjoyable. Much to the chagrin of the airlines, people in the industry don't travel to nearly the extent that management consultants do.

Compensation

Compensation in the brokerage and asset management industries can be heady. Throughout the industry, compensation is performance-based in one way or another. For portfolio managers and their groups, compensation centers around a lucrative base salary capped by bonuses for fund or company performance. Traders receive bonuses based on how well they execute trades. In the case of stockbrokers, compensation can be 100 percent performance-based. Private bankers who bring in wealthy clients generally receive a percentage of assets, fees, or both, but they might not get that all in one lump sum. In order to encourage bankers to keep clients' assets with the firm, payment for bringing in clients often gets split up over time like an annuity.

RETAIL STOCKBROKERS AND FINANCIAL ADVISORS

Compensation structures in the retail brokerage industry take on a limited number of forms. Broadly speaking, brokers are salaried or receive commission-based compensation. The firms that offer base salary after initial training are limited, by and large, to the discount brokerage and bank financial planning realms.

Traditional brokerage firms, on the other hand, usually pay brokers on a purely commission basis after a specified time or after a period of training. At Edward Jones, the company pays for training and offers a salary of $1,820 a month for one year ("standard performance," with bonuses and commissions, will earn you about $55,000 during that time). The broker commission, known as a *payout rate* in the industry, is based on management fees or transaction fees from stock purchases and sales. Typically, a national brokerage firm will pay you 36 to 40 percent of gross fees you earn from your clients. Additionally, the firm will cover expenses such as rent for the office, administrative support, local marketing costs, and some office supplies. Independent brokerages offer their advisors payouts as high as 90 percent (or higher), but in exchange for this liberty, the advisors have to pay for the entire office infrastructure themselves. For most independent brokers, this brings their payout rate to about the same percentage as that of national brokerages.

Seasoned brokers are in high demand currently. Lots of registered reps are making in excess of $200,000 annually in the current market, with some earning in excess of a million bucks a year. Be aware, though, that it's slim pickings until you build a client base. Starting out, you could earn less than $40,000. And a downward turn in the markets usually hurts everyone's bottom line, investors and brokers alike.

MUTUAL FUNDS

The top fund managers of the biggest funds earn basis points on the management fee the fund charges investors, so the more money they manage, the more money they make. Managers of high-performing funds can make $10 million to $15 million a year. Salaries for index fund managers, who maintain funds intended to mirror the performance of a particular market index, usually top out at around $200,000.

HEDGE FUNDS

Hedge fund managers can make some serious bank. According to one hedge fund insider, the average fund manager earns $400,000 per year, but managers at some funds can make much, much more. In addition to a management fee of 1 to 2 percent of assets, hedge funds tend to take a percentage of profits (should there be any), generally to the tune of 20 percent. So the top hedge fund managers can become quite wealthy. The median starting salary for top MBAs is $100,000.

Asset Management Salaries

Position	Salary Range
Fund manager	$200,000 to >$1 million
Junior analyst	$60,000 to $100,000
Customer representative/back office	$30,000 to $100,000
Compliance officer	$45,000 to $150,000
Fund relationship manager	$100,000 to $175,000
Fund sales	$150,000 to $500,000

Source: WetFeet research

Vacation, Benefits, and Perks

Asset management and brokerage firms have the distinct advantage of being tied to the Wall Street calendar. The New York Stock Exchange has nine holidays a year; most retail brokerage and asset management firms follow suit. In general, vacation, perquisites, and benefits are excellent in the industry. Vacation varies from as few as two weeks to as many as four or five weeks. Foreign-based companies with significant U.S. operations are especially generous when it comes to vacation.

Many companies are keenly aware of work/life balance and offer benefits such as flex-time, domestic partner benefits, tuition reimbursement, and reimbursement for "life cycle" events such as childbirth classes and home fitness. American Century dangles the carrot of a four-week paid sabbatical for employees who have served seven years.

Most companies will also spring for industry training—such as for Series 7 classes and testing. Referral bonus programs are also ubiquitous among top-tier firms.

Finally, the industry does not forget that it is in the wealth creation business: 401(k) and retirement plans are among the best around. Employer matching in 401(k) programs is ubiquitous. Vanguard's Retirement and Savings Plan allows its "crew" to invest a portion of their income in Vanguard funds and receive additional contributions from the fund giant.

Career Path

OPPORTUNITIES FOR UNDERGRADUATES

Unless you have an uncle who wants to bring you in under his wing, you probably won't get into a retail brokerage trainee program. There are exceptions, however; Edward Jones, for example, is noted for bringing undergrads with little work experience into its training program. Discount brokerages offer opportunities in customer service that can lead to advisory positions. In the majority of asset management firms, you are most likely to get a job involving a lot of phone time with clients, either as an investment service representative or as a salesperson. An industry insider describes his first job out of college as glorified data entry, inputting trades into the computer system. But these positions can help you gain essential product and market knowledge, as well as hone your skills interacting with investors. This experience can position you for a move into management, where you can influence the direction and character of the firm. Those who develop a comprehensive understanding of the whole process and can improve any weak links in the organization will definitely be able to move up. There's no up-or-out policy, and there are opportunities across the board, but sales has the biggest potential for fast advancement.

Some other firms also bring undergrads into retail brokerage positions. Merrill Lynch, for instance, starts recent grads as analysts in its private client group before moving successful employees to other positions in the division. Insiders also recommend doing an investment banking analyst program to get some Wall Street cred (read: analytical skills and industry knowledge) before trying to break into portfolio management.

OPPORTUNITIES FOR MBAS

MBAs will also have a tough time getting into a retail brokerage training program. You may be sharp, but unless you have a few years of solid real-world success behind you (preferably in sales), the brokerage firms don't want to take the risk. At mutual funds, investment counseling firms, and bank trust departments, many MBAs perform research and analysis that contributes to the work of various teams and portfolio managers who are ultimately responsible for the performance of different funds. In some exceptional cases, a talented MBA can sign on as a fund manager, but hot MBAs are more likely to come in as analysts or assistant fund managers. You will gain increasing responsibility as you demonstrate an understanding of the market and make more significant contributions. And, if you're really, really good, there are millions of dollars out there with your name on them.

OPPORTUNITIES FOR MIDCAREER CANDIDATES

In asset management firms, there are more midcareer opportunities in sales, marketing, and administration than in research and portfolio management. Sales, marketing, and administrative skills are more transferable from other industries; analysis and asset management are more specialized, and managers tend to be groomed (not cloned) from within the company.

If you're seeking to get into the retail brokerage industry, success in your first career—be it law, accounting, education, management, sales, or medicine—will give you a huge leg up over a young hotshot MBA. Brokerage firms want maturity, experience, and proven entrepreneurial success.

Insider Scoop

WHAT EMPLOYEES REALLY LIKE

Compensation

Salaries and bonuses in the current market climate aren't setting any records, but then again, not many fund managers are on food stamps. Those who still have jobs are generally well compensated, and when the market turns around, as inevitably it must, Porsche Boxster– and "house in the Hamptons"–sized bonuses are sure to return to top portfolio and fund managers. Sales positions can also command hefty bonuses in good times, but nothing like those of I-banking salespeople and traders.

The Challenge

The market has a thousand faces and shows you a new one each day. It can take a lifetime to feel you have any kind of handle on it. Many insiders report that the intellectual challenge—trying to be smarter than the market—keeps their jobs forever interesting. "If you like it, it's a fun game; the smartest people in the world do it," says one insider. "It's like poker except the stakes are a lot bigger." Analysts enjoy the challenge of unraveling a numeric puzzle. And for salespeople, it's all about closing the deal.

Variety of Opportunities

No matter where you start in the asset management business, there are many avenues you can pursue depending on how your interests develop. If marketing is your forte, you can develop and launch new products and services to keep investment dollars coming in. If managing money is your hot button, you can start by doing research and work into an investment management position. You can move from a bank trust department to a mutual fund. You can get into retail brokerage or start your own hedge fund. With a proven ability to make money, there will always be investors willing to pay you to manage theirs.

Less Cutthroat than I-Banking or Consulting

Stability is a quality that most investors desire in an asset management company. Insiders tell us that many asset management companies don't like to lose employees and will create multiple career paths to retain trusted talent. Whereas I-banks have short-term horizons for deals, and consulting firms have similarly time-bound projects, investment counseling firms and mutual fund companies have long-term goals of maintaining their investors' principal and increasing returns with as little risk as possible. These goals translate into a generally more relaxed environment and less of a sink-or-swim mentality. "It's the quality of life," says one insider of a large firm's financial advisor group. "You have the ability to make money and see your family. And it's not the type of environment where you don't have a career path after a few years."

High-Level Contacts

Mutual fund and portfolio managers with a lot of investment money to throw around will find that CEOs of top companies come calling to talk up their operations. Managers, analysts, and researchers have the chance to meet these bigwigs in small, face-to-face meetings and ask them lots of questions that CEOs might otherwise be reluctant to answer. Take notes.

High Visibility

While fame may be too strong a word, top asset managers can attain something like celebrity status within the investment community. If you're well-spoken and stock-savvy, financial news shows and publications will gladly pick your brain on the air or in print—though you might think twice before giving away your biggest trade secrets. You know you're somebody when a caricature of your mug appears on the cover of *Barron's*.

Helping People

When you help people make money, they are very, very appreciative. A lot of people are lost in the wilderness when it comes to financial management, and they're thankful for someone who can show them the way. A retail broker has direct contact with his clients, and close relationships can develop. A mutual fund manager may not meet with John Q. Investor, but a good one never forgets the investors she serves.

WATCH OUT!

Stock Market Volatility

Until recently, there were plenty of professionals out there who had never experienced a real bear market. And now they have. You lose money, your clients lose money, your firm loses money, investors pull out of the market, and ultimately a lot of people lose their jobs. If you're a broker and you have to explain to a client why he may have to postpone retirement for a few years, it's not pretty. If you're one of the unfortunates who gets laid off in a bear market, you may find yourself mixing drinks for your old colleagues until the market turns around. And if you're a savvy fund manager who continues to beat the major indices simply by losing less than they are, you may not experience the same satisfaction as you would in a growing market.

Performance Anxiety

Fund or portfolio performance is the key factor for a company's success, and the pressure to perform is high—maybe too high. Hedge funds often update their investors on a monthly or even weekly basis, increasing the chance that a bad spell—even if short—will send assets out the door. "Investors have quick trigger fingers," said one insider.

Investors have so many choices and can make changes to different funds so quickly and cheaply that funds are coming under pressure both to keep costs way down and to beat the market consistently. This in turn puts a lot of pressure on fund managers who are making intelligent bets that can lose no matter how smart they are. Retail brokers are entrusted with the life savings, the retirement plans, the college funds—in short, the dreams—of their clients. If you don't feel that pressure in a bear market, you have ice in your veins.

Internal Competition

Internal competition is not always a negative, but you have to watch out for the degree to which it exists and the way it influences a person's behavior. If there's a real cannibal culture where one person or department is going to lose power or stature when another does better, it can be very discouraging. The level of politics also rises correspondingly. Just look at recent headlines in the business section to see what greed can do to people.

Where Did My Life Go?

Asset management is less demanding than I-banking or management consulting, but you're still going to have to work hard for your money. You'll want to be at the office bright and early before the market opens to see what's happening in *The Wall Street Journal* and prepare for the day's action. If you work in California, expect to roll in bright and early at 5:00 a.m. "The biggest downside is that the job never ends," says one insider. "Even when you're on vacation, the market is running. I call on the traders a few times a day to make sure positions don't blow up."

International fund managers are particularly hard-pressed, because so much of their business is conducted overseas. That can mean long trips and meetings scheduled according to Singapore time. If you're an analyst or manager, there's always one more thing you should read, one more fact to know. That can be tough on people who don't know how to call it quits.

Unstable Ground

Merger activity among financial firms has been frantic in the past few years. Both in the United States and in other countries, all types of consolidations, purchases, and takeovers are changing the makeup of financial institutions, including mutual funds. Many mergers today are based on cost savings, and that means job cutting. So along with market volatility, these activities increase the pink-slip factor.

Slow to Change

Investment companies often have difficulty changing processes and procedures. Perhaps this is because companies must strive so hard to create a sense of stability in the midst of constantly changing markets. Insiders report some mutual fund companies have also had an ongoing problem integrating new technology—spending hundreds of millions of dollars on systems that have become part of an unmanageable patchwork of computers.

Getting Hired

Requirements

The Recruiting Process

Interviewing Tips

Getting Grilled

Grilling Your Interviewer

Requirements

Undergraduates with their hearts set on a career in asset management should take as many statistics and accounting classes as possible to prove that they can handle all of the number crunching and financial modeling that the profession requires. Undergraduates may be able to land jobs as research analysts, though competition is tough and they may be going up against candidates with MBAs.

If you're really serious about the profession, start with a job in sales, marketing, operations, or trading at an asset management firm, then consider going back for an MBA or taking your CFA before switching into asset management per se. You may also consider a two-year analyst or research position in investment banking. Such jobs are more plentiful and provide excellent training for asset management.

MBAs usually come aboard as researchers or analysts. Analysts and researchers generally serve at least two years before they come up for consideration as fund managers. It's important to note, however, that not all asset management firms see the MBA as a key to success. The degree "is not that important for portfolio management," said one insider. "If you want to become a manager and run a marketing program, then perhaps it's useful. The CFA is the designation given the most reverence in asset management."

You are more likely to get an asset manager position earlier if you run smaller portfolios for institutional asset managers or private banks that offer services to the wealthy. On the mutual fund side, you might become portfolio co-manager, sharing the management responsibility with a senior manager. The larger the pool of assets, the fiercer the competition.

There is no single prerequisite to becoming an asset manager or broker. It all comes down to how much money you can make with other people's money. That said, virtually all successful asset managers and brokers possess the following skills:

QUANTITATIVE AND ANALYTICAL SKILLS

Asset managers have to be able to read spreadsheets and earnings reports. And they have to be able to take those numbers and crunch them into financial models and projections. Even if you're dealing with less volatile investments such as bonds or real estate, you have to do the math to stay ahead of conventional wisdom. Classes in accounting and statistics are a big help, as are jobs that require number crunching, from I-banking to management consulting.

MANAGERIAL AND ORGANIZATIONAL SKILLS

Whether you're a researcher or a fund manager, you'll have to keep track of reams of facts from which to glean the really important information. Furthermore, you'll have to be able to make decisions—and execute them—quickly and accurately. Delay can cost big money. Finally, you need to be able to motivate and manage a talented staff of researchers and analysts if you work your way up to portfolio manager. Without their coordinated efforts, you may not have the information you need to make the best decision possible. "Solid general management experience is always in demand," says a recruiter. "There is such an opportunity for financial success without managing people at all that many professionals don't do it, don't want it, and don't develop the skills."

PROFESSIONAL LICENSING

In general, asset managers who work behind the scenes and make the big decisions don't need professional licensing. But if you're dealing with the public at all, you probably will, especially if you're in a position to make buy and sell recommendations directly to a client. For example, you may need one or more NASD licenses (Series 7, 63, or 65), or certain insurance licenses. Employers will generally give you the time to get such licenses once you're hired and may even pay the costs.

Becoming a broker is a bit different from becoming an asset manager. For one thing, there are a lot more jobs for brokers than for fund managers, so launching a brokerage career can be somewhat easier than becoming a fund manager. Brokers need to have quantitative and analytical skills in order to understand whether a given investment is attractive or not, but often not to the same degree as asset management pros. They also need to be professionally licensed, usually by passing the Series 7 and Series 63 exams. The big difference is that, while asset managers don't usually have much contact with the people investing in the funds they manage (especially in the case of retail investors), being a broker is all about dealing with investors. You've got to have some pretty serious sales ability, and relationship-management skills, to make it as a broker.

The Recruiting Process

Fidelity, Merrill Lynch, Deutsche Bank, Raymond James, Credit Suisse, and Vanguard are among the many diverse asset management companies and brokerage firms that recruit on campus. It can really pay off to interview with several of the major firms, but you should also dig up a few smaller alternatives where you might get on a faster track to more responsibility with less structure. If a company you've got your sights on doesn't recruit on campus, which often happens if no alums are working at the firm, it's best to know someone. "You have to have friends in the industry who can make sure they look at your resume."

UNDERGRADUATES

Undergraduates from all disciplines are hired into asset management companies. The best option is to check job listings and company websites and contact the company directly. If you can impress on a mutual fund recruiter that you value the customer and can be trained to use the computer system to access account and market information, you can start in a sales capacity and get a basic understanding of the business by training on the job. From there you can talk to people in other departments to find additional areas of interest.

MBAS

If your goal is to manage money, you need to select asset management companies you think you might want to work for and start networking. The selection process for portfolio managers is formal and very competitive. It's less formal but still selective for other positions. You need to find out what particular qualities a company is looking for. The more you understand a particular company's investment philosophy and can discuss it intelligently while networking and interviewing, the more likely the company will take an interest in you as a potential hire. There is some campus recruitment for portfolio managers, analysts, and researchers, but the companies also hire through local advertisements and headhunters. Strong academic credentials and demonstrated market knowledge are musts.

MIDCAREER CANDIDATES

Midcareer professionals can reap big returns in sales positions and may be prime candidates for retail brokerage training programs. For these jobs, you will have to go through the rigmarole of getting a Series 7 license—not a cakewalk, but not the bar exam either. A marketing background is easily transferable into a marketing position in the financial industry. Check job listings, search company websites, and make direct contact with the firms of your choice to get your foot in the interviewer's door.

Interviewing Tips

Because the market has posted terrific gains over the past couple of years, recruiting is picking up—but competition for top-shelf jobs is still fierce. Research your potential candidates well and follow these tips:

1. The asset management industry loves teamwork. You'll make a better impression if you talk about your values, your work ethic, and the importance of teamwork rather than your love of the spotlight.

2. Different firms in different cities all have their own distinctive character and style. Research the culture and be able to articulate how you'll fit in.

3. For portfolio manager, analyst, and researcher positions, be conversant with investment theories and models such as CAPM (capital asset pricing model) and *Graham and Dodd's Security Analysis*, the classic textbook on value investing. Discuss industries where you have specific knowledge. Reveal your best stock picks and your dream portfolio.

4. Be yourself, but be direct. Be able to communicate your work experience and educational highlights in 30- or 60-second sound bites. This is a valued skill in an industry where the ability to summarize information quickly and accurately is so important.

5. Remember that behind all of the charts and graphs there is an investor, the customer. Let your interviewer know that you understand how important that person is.

6. The investment industry is, after all the research and analysis is done, about opinions. Both for retail brokers and research analysts, presenting an aura of confidence and authority is critical for success.

Getting Grilled

While the investment industry is vast and job functions vary greatly, the following will give you some idea of the range of questions that interviewers commonly ask. Those in the "Rare" section are innocuous, while the "Well Done" questions will prove more difficult to answer.

RARE

- What are your greatest strengths?

- What are your greatest weaknesses?

- What role do you play in team projects?

- Where do you want to be in five years?

- What accomplishment are you most proud of?

- Why do you want to work at [company name]?

- What about the industry interests you?

- How do you like to spend your free time?

MEDIUM

- Tell me about a stock you would recommend.

- How do you keep informed about the financial markets?

- How would you value Company X?

- What are the primary differences in valuing companies in industry X versus industry Y?

- What sectors do you like now?

- Describe your ideal job.

- What stocks are you following?

WELL DONE

- Why should we hire you?

- Why are you interested in asset management instead of investment banking?

- Tell me about a time you failed.

- Give me an example of a time when one of your investment decisions failed. How did you handle it?

- What political and economic factors are affecting financial markets?

- How do you see our firm as we relate to competitors?

- What will happen to bond prices if interest rates fall/rise?

- How do you know you can sell?

Grilling Your Interviewer

This is your chance to turn the tables and find out what you really want to know about the asset management and retail brokerage industry. The following generic questions will fit most industry interviews, but you'll no doubt want to come up with a few of your own. Again, those in the "Rare" section are meant to be innocuous, while the "Well Done" questions will put fire under your interviewer's feet.

RARE

- What is the company culture like? What kinds of people do well here?

- Is there a career path or formal channel of advancement?

- What is the bonus structure, and what is the company's history of paying bonuses?

- Is it difficult to transfer to other departments in the company?

MEDIUM

- What new developments do you see in the next year and beyond?

- What training and educational options do you offer and pay for?

- Do you stick to one investment philosophy?

- Can I trade my own account?

WELL DONE

- Do you monitor or record telephone conversations with clients?

- Is there any bias you've observed in the promotional process?

- Are there any unwritten rules?

- What do you think of Ben Bernanke? (Look it up if you don't already know who this guy is.)

For Your Reference

Industry Lingo

Articles

Books

Online References

Industry Lingo

The following terms are common to the brokerage and asset management industries. Based on our interviews with insiders, we selected terms that are appropriate to these industries, as well as those that are critical to an understanding of the broader financial services field. See the "Online Glossaries" section for a list of additional resources you can look to for any industry terms not included here.

10-K. Annual report required of public companies by the SEC. The 10-K contains more detailed financial information and descriptions of a company's business and business risk than does the glossy, but comparatively milquetoast, annual report. Foreign companies file annual reports that are submitted as form 20-F.

10-Q. Quarterly report required of public firms by the SEC.

12B-1 fees. Fees collected by some mutual funds based on a percentage of assets and share price.

401(k). A plan offered by a corporation to individuals to allow them to save for retirement.

Advisor. A person or company responsible for investing fund assets.

Active investment. An investment by a fund manager that seeks to outperform market indices.

Alpha. The coefficient of risk-adjusted performance for a security, rather than volatility compared to the overall market (beta). Alpha is used to measure absolute performance and is beginning to become a popular measure of mutual fund performance, as it offers a measure of performance compared to an unmanaged portfolio of the same risk level. Portfolios with a positive alpha are performing better than unmanaged portfolios; those with negative alphas are performing worse.

Arbitrage. The practice of taking advantage of price differentials among securities to profit from market inefficiencies.

Asset. Any item with economic value that can be sold for cash.

Back office. The operations of a brokerage that process and report transactions. Many asset management companies concentrate on investing and outsource back-office operations to companies like State Street.

Bar. Industry parlance for a million units of currency.

Beta. The measure of volatility of a stock in comparison to the general market. A stock with a beta of 1 will have the same volatility as the market. A stock with a beta greater than 1, such as a biotech startup, will have greater volatility—sort of a manic-depressive personality with higher highs and lower lows. A sleepy old dog of a stock like a utility might have a beta of less than 1 and therefore less volatility than the overall market.

Bid. The price a buyer is willing to pay for a security.

Block trade. The sale or purchase of a large number of shares of a security.

Buy-side analyst. A securities analyst who is employed by an asset management firm, mutual fund, or similar entity that invests in its own accounts. Unlike sell-side analysts, buy-side analysts cover multiple firms within multiple industries.

Call option. The option to purchase a security at a set price in the future.

Capital market. Market where companies and governments go to raise capital through the sale of medium- and long-range securities.

Chartered Financial Analyst (CFA). An industry credential administered by CFA Institute (formerly the AIMR), a nonprofit association of more than 75,000 investment professionals from 117 countries. The CFA credential requires at least three years of professional investment experience, successful completion of three six-hour tests over two years, and commitment to an ethical code of conduct.

Chinese wall. A procedure in a brokerage firm put in place to keep groups that have insider or market-sensitive information from sharing that information outside the group.

Closed-end fund. A mutual fund with a fixed number of shares that is often traded on an exchange.

Dealer. A person or company buying securities for their own account.

Derivative. Any financial instrument whose value is derived from an underlying asset such as a stock, bond, currency, market, or market index. For instance, a *call* or *put option* (see entry following) on a stock is a derivative.

Desk. A department in a brokerage firm or asset management company that trades a particular type of security. For instance, a trader may be on the high-yield desk or the options desk.

Equity. Describes any security that has an ownership interest in a company, most often a stock.

Expense ratio. Metric that measures the costs associated with managing and running a fund.

Feeder fund. Similar to a fund of funds, a feeder fund does all of its business through other funds. It is often used to give domestic investors the tax advantages of investing in foreign funds.

Fixed-income security. Any security that pays a set interest rate, including bonds, money market instruments, and preferred stock.

Front loaded mutual fund. A fund in which management fees are paid at the time of purchase.

Fund of funds. A fund that invests in other funds. Funds of funds are especially popular in the hedge fund world, where the fund of funds manager can manage risk by taking advantage of the investment styles of many different hedge fund managers.

Fundamental analysis. Market analysis based on macroeconomic factors such as large-scale supply and demand, as well as a company's financial statements.

Hedge fund. A fund that is less regulated by the SEC and therefore can use instruments that are unavailable to mutual funds and traditional funds, such as program trading, derivatives, short positions, leverage, and arbitrage. Hedge funds are said to be uncorrelated to market movements.

High-yield security. A below-investment-grade security, also known as a *junk bond*, which offers the buyer a high yield in exchange for increased risk.

Index fund. A mutual fund whose portfolio is composed of securities in the same proportions as a major stock index.

Institutional investor. An investor or company that invests on behalf of another organization, such as an insurance company or pension fund.

Leverage. The use of borrowed money to purchase securities. Hedge funds often use leverage as an investment tool.

Load fund. A fund whose shares are sold with a fee at the time of purchase or redemption of shares.

Offer. The price at which a seller is willing to sell a security.

Over the counter (OTC). An informal market set up by dealers to trade securities not listed on major exchanges.

Passive investment. An investment, such as an index fund, that seeks to mirror performance of a market index by constructing a portfolio that mirrors that of the index.

Payout. The percentage of a customer commission or service fee that a retail stockbroker receives. Stockbrokers with major brokerage firms receive around 40 percent, whereas independent brokers receive substantially higher rates, up to nearly 100 percent, but might have to pay for their own offices, assistants, and transaction processing fees.

Pension. Compensation an employee receives after he or she has retired.

Portfolio. The composition of a fund, which may contain any combination of stocks, bonds, and money market investments.

Portfolio trade. A trade in which a portfolio manager sells a number of different portfolio securities to rebalance the portfolio.

Primary market. The market in which securities are initially offered to buyers, for instance an IPO or a debt issuance.

Prime broker. A broker that settles trades and provides custody services for a client as well as loans securities and provides loans. Hedge funds are big clients of prime brokers such as Goldman Sachs.

Program trading. Automated trading based on computer models that take advantage of price discrepancies between markets and securities.

Put option. The option to sell a security at a given price in the future.

Secondary market. The market for securities after initial distribution.

Security. Any financial instrument that shows evidence of ownership of a stock or bond.

Sell-side analyst. A securities analyst employed by an investment bank, brokerage firm, or independent company who researches and recommends securities, usually within a single industry.

Series 63. State required license to become a stockbroker. Not all states require a Series 63 license.

Series 7. License required to sell all types of securities and therefore to be a stockbroker or financial advisor. The Series 7 is the SAT of the financial services industry. The test runs six hours and consists of 250 questions covering debt and equities securities, options and derivatives, securities regulation, retirement plans, investment companies, taxation, and financial analysis. Many brokerage firms will pay for training for their employees.

Stockbroker. A person who buys and sells stocks on behalf of a client.

Taft-Hartley plan. A multiemployer pension plan established under the sweeping labor legislation of 1947 known as the Taft-Hartley Act. A Taft-Hartley plan allows workers to gain credit for pensions while working for many different employers, as defined by collective bargaining agreements. Essentially a labor union fund. The Teamsters' pension plans are governed by Taft-Hartley legislation.

Technical analysis. Analysis based purely on historical stock and market price data.

Trader. A person who buys and sells securities for his or her own account.

Wirehouse. A large, national brokerage firm (named so because wirehouse firms used to be connected to one another electronically), as opposed to an independent brokerage.

Yield curve. The relationship between short-term and long-term interest rates, expressed graphically. The X-axis represents the maturation term, with short-term rates on the left and longer terms toward the right. The Y-axis denotes the interest rate.

Articles

"Broker Job-Hopping Raises Concerns"

A look at how the demand for brokers caused by recent strong market performance has resulted in lots of brokerage turnover and some pretty hefty compensation packages.

Jane J. Kim, *The Wall Street Journal,* **May 25, 2006**

"Alphabet Soup: Financial Advisors Are Adding More Titles to Their Business Cards"

A look at the distinctions between the 35 or so different designations for financial services and investment advisory professionals, including the CFP, ChFC, PFS, and RIA.

Karen Hube, *The Wall Street Journal,* **April 24, 2006**

"Goldman Gurus Strike It Rich with Hedge Fund"

A look at a successful Goldman Sachs hedge fund operation.

Randall Smith, *The Wall Street Journal,* **April 20, 2006**

"Your Money Manager as Financial Therapist"

More and more brokers and financial planners are finding that devoting more personalized attention to clients pays off.

Lingling Wei, *The Wall Street Journal,* **November 11, 2005**

"Northern Trust's New Wanderlust"

The Midwestern wealth manager does its Grand Tour.

Adrienne Carter, *BusinessWeek,* **April 11, 2005**

"The Busiest Broker on Earth"

Fidelity Investments stealthily ramps up its online brokerage to pressure rivals Charles Schwab and Merrill Lynch.

Aaron Pressman, *BusinessWeek***, April 7, 2005**

"Lazard's Clash of the Titans"

Details the power struggle between Lazard's French partners and brash American dealmaker Bruce Wasserstein leading up to the venerable investment bank's 2005 IPO.

Vicky Ward, *Vanity Fair***, April 2005**

"Wall Street on the Run"

Describes how Eliot Spitzer is single-handedly changing the business model of sell-side analysts.

Andrew Nocera, *Fortune***, June 14, 2004**

"Are Hedge Funds Too Good To Be True?"

Describes the lure of hedge funds and the lack of regulation surrounding them.

Faith Arner, *BusinessWeek***, May 10, 2004**

"Eddie Stern's Passion"

A lurid insider tale of the mutual fund scandal.

Peter Elkind, *Fortune***, April 19, 2004**

"The House Always Wins"

Gary Pilgrim turns his fund into a money machine for himself.

John Helyar, *Fortune***, March 8, 2004**

"Can Sallie Save Citi?"

Thirty-eight-year-old Sallie Krawcheck is named CEO of Smith Barney. The article outlines issues facing the retail brokerage industry as well as gives a profile of the ex–Sanford C. Bernstein analyst.

David Rynecki, *Fortune,* **May 27, 2003**

"Wall Street's Secret Power Elite: Where the Money Is Really Made"

A summary of the current state of the hedge fund industry.

Andy Serwer, *Fortune,* **March 17, 2003**

Books

Reminiscences of a Stock Operator

Originally published in 1923, *Reminiscences* is the biography of Jesse Livermore, one of the greatest speculators of all time. Traders of all stripes consider this one of the all-time best accounts of trading life.

Edwin LeFevre (Wiley, 2006)

Valuation: Measuring and Managing the Value of Companies

McKinsey's take on valuation techniques, a good primer on valuing companies for budding analysts.

Tim Koller, Marc Goedhart, and David Wessels (Wiley, 2005)

The Intelligent Investor: The Definitive Book on Value Investing

Originally published in 1949, Graham's book has remained the most respected guide to investing due to his timeless philosophy of "value investing."

Benjamin Graham (Collins, 2003)

The Mutual Fund Business

The first textbook devoted exclusively to the mutual fund industry.

Robert C. Pozen (Houghton Mifflin, 2002)

When Genius Failed: The Rise and Fall of Long-Term Capital Management

A look inside one of the most famous and infamous hedge funds of all time and one that had on its staff none other than Nobel Prize–winning economist and inventor of the Black-Scholes model, Myron Scholes. The book gives insight not only into how hedge funds work, but the culture within them.

Roger Lowenstein (Random House, 2001)

Fidelity's World: The Secret Life and Public Power of the Mutual Fund Giant

An outsider's look at Fidelity, by a *New York Times* reporter whom management wouldn't talk to.

Diana B. Henriques (Touchstone, 1997)

The Morningstar Approach to Investing

This respected mutual fund research organization gives a detailed look at funds and their managers.

Andrew Lecky (Warner Books, 1997)

Security Analysis: The Classic 1934 Edition

The definitive text on value investing written by Warren Buffett's mentor. Graham and Dodd wrote the book in 1934, after the (other) bubble had burst. Their approach to investing is deeply colored by this bust. Note that this 725-page monster is somewhat difficult to read for those without some understanding of accounting.

Benjamin Graham and David L. Dodd (McGraw-Hill, 1996)

The Vanguard Experiment: John Bogle's Quest to Transform the Mutual Fund Industry

Structured as a not-for-profit entity, John Bogle's company attracts some of the brightest talent around. Vanguard popularized the investment index.

Robert Slater (McGraw-Hill Trade, 1996)

Buffett: The Making of an American Capitalist

A biography of legendary value investor Warren Buffett.

Roger Lowenstein (Main Street Books, 1996)

Beating the Street

The author, Peter Lynch, beat the Street more consistently than most managers and propelled Magellan to international fame and fortune.

Peter Lynch (Fireside, 1994)

Liar's Poker: Rising Through the Wreckage on Wall Street

Wall Street is one big game, and this hilarious and irreverent look at what it's really like to play in it is a must-read for all those who aspire to be players themselves.

Michael Lewis (Penguin USA, 1990)

Online References

- **Investment Company Institute** (www.ici.org): An association of mutual fund companies. The site offers information about the organization of mutual funds, a mutual fund handbook, as well as copious statistics about the mutual fund industry.

- **Investorside Research Association** (www.investorside.org): An association of independent research firms.

- *Pensions & Investments* (www.pionline.com): Pensions & Investments magazine's online presence. Contains industry news and statistics.

- *Institutional Investor* (www.dailyii.com): A subscriber site for the institutional investor community, with some free content, including news.

- **Hedge Fund Association** (www.thehfa.org): Loose hedge fund industry association. It has some information about member companies and hedge fund investment strategies.

- **NASD** (www.nasd.com): Contains resources, glossaries, and investment information from the NASD, the self-regulating organization for the securities industry.

- **NASD Rules & Regulation** (www.nasdr.com): Contains information on all the examinations (Series 7, etc.) administered by the NASD.

- **New York Stock Exchange** (www.nyse.com): The NYSE has a number of good resources that provide a background on how the market works and the anatomy of a trade.

ONLINE GLOSSARIES

General Terms

- www.investorwords.com: a general glossary of financial terms

Brokerage and Trading Terms

- http://www.nasd.com/Resources/Glossary/index.htm: NASD glossary

- www.trading-glossary.com: glossary of trading terms sponsored by the Highlight Investments Group

Hedge Fund Terms

- www.russell.com/II/Research_and_Resources/Alternative_Investing/Hedge_Fund_Glossary.asp: Russell Institutional Investors' hedge fund glossary—full of arcane hedge fund terms

Mutual Fund Terms

- www.investopedia.com/categories/mutualfunds.asp: glossary of mutual funds terms

WETFEET'S INSIDER GUIDE SERIES

Job Search Guides

Be Your Own Boss

Changing Course, Changing Careers

Finding the Right Career Path

Getting Your Ideal Internship

International MBA Student's Guide to the U.S. Job Search

Job Hunting A to Z: Landing the Job You Want

Killer Consulting Resumes!

Killer Cover Letters & Resumes!

Killer Investment Banking Resumes!

Negotiating Your Salary & Perks

Networking Works!

Interview Guides

Ace Your Case®: Consulting Interviews

Ace Your Case® II: 15 More Consulting Cases

Ace Your Case® III: Practice Makes Perfect

Ace Your Case® IV: The Latest & Greatest

Ace Your Case® V: Return to the Case Interview

Ace Your Case® VI: Mastering the Case Interview

Ace Your Interview!

Beat the Street®: Investment Banking Interviews

Beat the Street® II: I-Banking Interview Practice Guide

Career & Industry Guides

Careers in Accounting

Careers in Advertising & Public Relations

Careers in Asset Management & Retail Brokerage

Careers in Biotech & Pharmaceuticals

Careers in Brand Management

Careers in Consumer Products

Careers in Entertainment & Sports

Careers in Health Care

Careers in Human Resources

Careers in Information Technology

Careers in Investment Banking

Careers in Management Consulting

Careers in Marketing & Market Research

Careers in Nonprofits & Government Agencies

Careers in Real Estate

Careers in Retail

Careers in Sales

Careers in Supply Chain Management

Careers in Venture Capital

Industries & Careers for MBAs

Industries & Careers for Undergrads

Million-Dollar Careers

Specialized Consulting Careers: Health Care, Human Resources, and Information Technology

Company Guides

25 Top Consulting Firms

25 Top Financial Services Firms

Accenture

Bain & Company

Booz Allen Hamilton

Boston Consulting Group

Credit Suisse First Boston

Deloitte Consulting

Deutsche Bank

The Goldman Sachs Group

JPMorgan Chase

McKinsey & Company

Merrill Lynch & Co.

Morgan Stanley

UBS AG

WetFeet in the City Guides

Job Hunting in New York City

Job Hunting in San Francisco